COTTON MATHER

KEEPER OF THE PURITAN CONSCIENCE

* ∞ *

The Life of men is full of Labour;
and it is generally a Labour
in Vain.
— The Diary of COTTON MATHER

COTTON MATHER

COTTON MATHER

KEEPER OF

THE PURITAN CONSCIENCE

By RALPH AND LOUISE BOAS

*With Illustrations from
Old Prints and Engravings*

ARCHON BOOKS
HAMDEN, CONNECTICUT
1964

COPYRIGHT, 1928, BY

RALPH PHILIP BOAS AND LOUISE SCHUTZ BOAS

REPRINTED, 1964, IN AN UNALTERED AND
UNABRIDGED EDITION BY ARRANGEMENT WITH
HARPER & ROW, INC.

LIBRARY OF CONGRESS CATALOG NUMBER: 64-15910
PRINTED IN THE UNITED STATES OF AMERICA

TO

RUDOLPH AND ESTHER SCHUTZ

INTRODUCTION

NEVER in American history has there been such interest in the New England Puritans as exists today. They are reviled as the source of all our woes and lauded as the only begetters of all our virtues. The name which they cherished as a symbol of their spotless devotion to religious truth has become a byword for repression, icy self-righteousness, and even morbid abnormality. Yet thousands of Americans count as their only distinction the fact that they can prove their descent from these men of iron will and assured faith. Bigotry and religious insight, savage persecution and political realism, niggardly self-righteousness and splendid morality — these and scores of antonyms are showered upon them.

But praise and detraction alike rest upon slender foundations. If the fame of the Puritans is firmly fixed in the minds of schoolboys, it is because of the romanticized legends of an age of pioneering; if it is anathema to " liberals," it is because of equally romanticized legends of mythical " blue laws."

Of all the Puritans, Cotton Mather is most often singled out for detraction. The years in which he lived, from 1663 to 1728, were the period of Puritanism midway between the romance of pioneering and the ardor of the revolutionary spirit. They have been lightly treated

[vii]

in history, and as a result the violent blame and the meager praise which have been given the most famous man of the period have been based upon but slender knowledge. Liberal New Englanders have hastened to disclaim any interest in either Cotton Mather or his father Increase Mather; men outside New England have been eager to defame them; and their defenders have often been interested in defending religious forms rather than personalities.

In this study we have tried to present a fair picture of the most famous Puritan of the middle period, with due regard to his social background in its various aspects. Students of the period will recognize the many and varied sources from which the material has been gathered; for the general reader, for whom this study is intended, minute citation of sources would serve no useful purpose.

The chapter on the Salem witchcraft, based upon a direct study of the multitude of sources available, presents a point of view for which the authors assume full responsibility.

ILLUSTRATIONS

COTTON MATHER

CHAPTER ONE

"... the Piety, the Erudition, the elegant Ability, the Sound Sense, the Prudence, and the
dignity of his GRANDFATHERS."
> — *President Oakes at Cotton Mather's
Commencement at Harvard*

I

ON April 16, 1669, there lay dying in his son's
house in Boston one of the last of a great generation, Richard Mather, minister of the church
at Dorchester. He was one of the breed who had left England to cross the Atlantic in a little tumbling ship for the
uncertainty of pioneer life in a frontier village. As he lay
in " a mortal extremity of pain " the pleasant scent of
English hedgerows in springtime replaced the pervasive
odor of the Boston mudflats, and the soothing touch of
moist winds off the North Sea softened the sharp north-
easter of a Boston April. He heard again the bitter voice
of the episcopal visitor refusing to reinstate him in the
Church of England; " for when the visitors had been informed that he had been a minister *fifteen* years, and all
that while never wore a *surpliss,* one of them swore,
' It had been better for him that he had gotten seven
bastards.' "

Dying, he was happy in the thought that he had given
the best years of a long life to God, and five sons to the
service of the church, the youngest and most distinguished

[1]

being Increase Mather, teacher of the North Church in Boston. The old man had lived a busy and useful life, quietly and unobtrusively upholding the cause of New England Congregationalism. In preaching he was a mighty man. " His voice was loud and big, and uttered with a deliberate vehemency; it procured unto his ministry an awful and very taking majesty." It was the authentic Mather voice, a deliberate " tonitrous cogency " in his son Increase; a " dilated deliberation " in his grandson Cotton. In 1669 this grandson, a boy of six, was old enough to understand to the full the dread spectacle of a Christian's deathbed.

He stood unnoticed in the corner of his grandfather's sick-room while servants hurried back and forth with basins and nauseating draughts; he listened while his father solemnly prepared the dying man for the imminent interview with God. In his childish mind he stored up this picture of a pious son exhorting a pious father; and with the normal child's love of imitation he projected himself into the years ahead, seeing himself a learned minister speeding his father's journey into the known Presence. Death to the Puritan led to no undiscovered country; it was but the doorway to the courtroom of a just Deity. The act of death involved more than the closing of eyes upon friends and life upon earth; it meant the gathering of all the evidence to plead before the final Judge one's right to a good hereafter because one had in feeble mortal fashion led a good life.

As Increase Mather discoursed with the dying man the small boy crept nearer to the bed. " Nunc dimittis " —

that, he knew, was the way learned men greeted death. He, too, would be a learned man; he, too, would preach to multitudes; he, too, when he was a man, would guide his father's footsteps on the path to heaven. Filled with admiration for these pious fathers of his, he hovered round the great bed so completely absorbing the scene that a morbid preoccupation with the idea of death was bred, a preoccupation that pursued him all his years.

And then the sick man began to plead for his home in Dorchester. He would see his beloved books once more; he would sit among them and perhaps finish one more literary labor; if he could only see them, touch them, he knew he could perform one more task for the Lord. He had never been an idler; he could not rest content even on his deathbed. " Take me home," he begged; then, casting off the weakness of disease, " Take me home," he commanded. And the small boy saw his father, that wise grown-up man, obey *his* father; and thus early he learned by direct example that a son's duty of obedience never ended while his parent breathed. Thus early he was set in the way he should go all his life — the idea of filial duty was fixed in his mind. It became the dominating influence of his life. It was not until he was, himself, almost at the end of his own mortal span that he actually sat by his father's deathbed; but now, child that he was, he saw himself there, deferring to his father's wishes, rounding out a life of obedience. Obedience to his father was the watchword of his entire life; at six he already saw its importance and its dignity.

At the funeral of Richard Mather the overwhelming

[3]

importance of death was further impressed upon him as he saw the honorary bearers solemn in black gloves and mourning rings march down the aisle to listen to the long sermon filled with eulogies of the dead and heavy reflections on eternity.

From this time on the boy Cotton was constantly watching for the angel of death. When he was old enough to keep a diary he constantly recorded — much as his father did in his diary — his belief that this was to be his last year on earth. He fully expected to die young; and the end of each year found him amazed at his continued residence on earth. He began to expect his father to die while that active man was yet comparatively young; when Increase reached seventy Cotton frequently prayed for and with him, hoping to prepare him better for his speedily approaching dissolution. But Increase rounded out eighty-four good years, dying, in fact, only five years before his devoted and overshadowed son.

Cotton Mather was not singular in his preoccupation with death. Intimate contact with death was part of the Puritan child's education. It was thought fitting that young children should be told frequently that they might at any moment be snatched from life; they might at any moment be suddenly hauled into the very presence of God, and made to answer for their brief lives. Cotton Mather himself, as a father, took occasion when two of his children had "newly been scorched with Gunpowder," but not seriously damaged, to talk to them about "their Danger of eternal Burnings." The modern parent, resting upon a philosophy none the less pessimistic

[4]

for its hedoniſtic ſtrain, feels apologetic for having thrust
life upon his offspring and therefore tries to thruſt happiness upon them. The seventeenth-century parent felt an
even ſtronger sense of duty toward his children; his task
it was to fit them to die.

More worldly men than the Mathers talked thus to
their ten-year-old sons: " Richard Dumer, a flourishing
youth of 9 years old, dies of the Small Pocks. I tell Sam.
of it and what need he had to prepare for Death, and
therefore to endeavour really to pray when he said over the
Lord's Prayer; He seem'd not much to mind, eating an
Aſple; but when he came to say, Our father, he burſt out
into a bitter Cry, and when I askt what was the matter
and he could speak, he burſt out into a bitter Cry and said
he was afraid he should die. I pray'd with him, and read
the Scriptures comforting againſt Death. . . . 'Twas at
noon."

Cotton Mather himself, in later years, when a fourteen-
year-old child was " crushed to Death, by a Cart falling
on him," felt that he should thereupon " preach a Sermon,
wherein Children shall be particularly and importunately
called upon, to prepare for the Day, wherein the Small
as well as the Great, shall ſtand before God."

When any one of his own children was ill he would
admonish the reſt " that they should be thankful to God
for their Health . . . ; And that they should be sensible
of their being obnoxious to the Early Stroke of Death, and
pray for Life, but prepare for Death."

Mather's Cotton grandfather had died too soon to
let his death preach for him, but the lesson of his life was

well taught by his daughter, Cotton Mather's mother, and by his widow doubly the boy's grandmother by her marriage to Richard Mather, a comfort for his old age. John Cotton, like Richard Mather, had been an immigrant in the epic age of Puritanism. As minister of the First Church at Boston he was a far more important man than the sage of Dorchester. " His excellent learning," cries the contemporary historian of the commonwealth, " profound judgment, eminent gravity, christian candour, and sweet temper of spirit . . . made him most desired when he was amongst them, and the more lamented, after he was removed hence. So equal a contention between learning and meekness, magnanimity and humility, is seldom seen in any one person. . . . He was a famous light in his generation, a glory to both Englands; one in whom was so much of what is desirable in man, as the consciences of all that knew him appealed unto, is rarely to be seen in any one conversant upon the earth." Leader of a church of which " some have been heard to say they believed . . . to be the most glorious church in the world," he was foremost in the banishment of Roger Williams and of Anne Hutchinson at a time when the Puritan theocracy was in the full sunlight of the stern Deity whom alone it respected. Yet John Cotton was a kind, good man, beloved of women and children, harsh only because to be kind to disturbers of God's peace meant destruction for all that the holiest men in the colony held most precious. Economic liberty belonged to every man, but political and religious liberty had to conform to John Winthrop's definition. " This liberty," wrote the famous governor,

" is the proper end and object of authority, and cannot subsist without it; and it is a liberty to that only which is good, just, and honest."

II

That Increase Mather, a young man of twenty-five when his first child, Cotton, was born, made the most of Richard Mather's death and John Cotton's reputation in training his young son in the right path, one may be sure, just as one may be sure that Cotton's birth on February 12, 1663, in the rigor of a Massachusetts winter, had not saved him from immediate baptism in a frigid church, though, as on another occasion, the sacramental bread were " frozen pretty hard, and rattled sadly as broken into the Plates." Delay was dangerous; although heaven was indeed the portion of few, at least a chance of Grace Everlasting might be besought for the child; and for the unbaptized hell was almost certain. The risk of pneumonia was less than that of hell; to die in the odor of sanctity was better than to live unregenerate. Hence proud young fathers held their infants in the chilly meeting-house, the ice was cracked in the christening bowl, and the babies' souls were given a chance.

For a time thereafter Cotton Mather's days had been peaceful. Like other babies in his station of life he had started his diet with a wet nurse (whom, many years later, he remembered to keep on his charity list). And he had been rocked and sung to sleep, for the Puritans had no aversion to the gentle craft of coddling babies. A later tale tells of a group of Quakers who came to the house of

[7]

a man inclined, against his wife's will, to join them. He was abroad, but nevertheless they sat them down, " humming and singing and groaning after their conjuring way — Says the woman are you singing quakers? yea, says they — Then take my squalling Brat of a child here and sing to it says she for I have almost split my throat with singing to him and cant get the Rogue to sleep."

As the first-born in an ample household Cotton Mather had no lack of attention. For a few years his young father complained bitterly to his diary that his congregation had little regard for his comfort; that his salary was inadequate for the demands of his growing family; and that he fell into debt. Increase Mather had refused a pastorate of four hundred pounds a year in England, returning to New England where such stipends were unknown. Nevertheless, the poverty he complained of was purely comparative. The men among whom he associated as an equal, and later as a leader, were practically all men of wealth. He was in the position of professional men today whose way of living requires a larger income than their salaries can possibly provide. The wives of men like Increase Mather were delicately bred; they could direct a household, but in their almost constant state of childbearing they needed nurses and servants. Their lyings-in were often but respites from attendance on sick and dying children. Many a young girl — like the first wife of Cotton Mather himself — married at sixteen and died at thirty-two, leaving but four of the nine children she had borne. Stronger women might have as many as twenty-two children, but nine or ten wore out most.

[8]

There is no description of Maria Mather, the mother of Cotton, but John Dunton, a bookseller, author, and publisher who, living in Boston in 1686, published an account of his travels in 1705, thus describes one Mrs. Green, a model — though probably imaginary — woman of New England: " as she is a good Wife to her Husband, so she is also a good Mother to her Children, whom she brings up with that sweetness and Facility as is admirable, not keeping them at too great a distance, (as some do) thereby Discouraging their good Parts; nor by an Over-Fondness (a fault most Mothers are guilty of) betraying 'em into a thousand Inconveniences, which oftentimes proves fatal to 'em.

" In brief she takes care of their Education, and whatever else belongs to 'em; so that Mr. Green enjoys the comfort of his Children, without knowing anything of the trouble of 'em.

" Nor is she less a Good Mistress than a good Mother; Treating her Servants with that Love and Gentleness as if she were their Mother; taking care both of their Souls and Bodies, and not letting them want anything necessary for either. I one Day told her, That I believ'd she was an extraordinary Wife; but Mr. Green was so good a Man, she cou'd not well be otherwise. To which she answer'd ' That she had so good a Husband, was her Mercy; but had her Husband been as bad a Man as any in the World, her Duty wou'd have been the same, and so she hop'd her Practice shou'd have been too.' Which, as it is a great Truth, it wants to be more known and Practic'd."

Servants — though good servants were scarce then as

now — had been brought over from the first to the Bay Colony, where, wrote Josselyn, a traveler who visited Boston in 1638 and again in 1663, " They have a store of Children, and are well accommodated with Servants; many hands make light work, many hands make a full fraught, but many mouths eat up all. . . ."

This was Increase Mather's difficulty. But servants were a necessity for men of his position and way of living, even though they were as unreliable as in a much later day when " servants bring followers and followers bring consequences, and consequences die a-teething." Twenty years later a contemporary noted in his diary: " Mr. Mather's Maid . . . is brought to Bed of a Child. Nothing suspected before that I hear of. 'Tis said he has turned her out of's house."

In 1645 a colonist had written: " I do not see how wee can thrive untill wee . . . gett a stock of slaves sufficient to do all our business." By 1663, according to Josselyn, there were both English and negro servants: " of the *English* there are can eat till they sweat, and work till they freeze; & of the females that are . . . very tender fingered in cold weather." The English were paid or indentured servants; the negroes were slaves, as were also the Indians. Of his Indian girl — bought on the deferred-payment plan, five pounds down and five pounds at the end of a year — the Reverend Mr. Peter Thatcher of Milton wrote in 1675 that she let the baby fall, " whereupon I took a good walnut stick and beat the Indian to purpose till she promised to do so no more." Cotton Mather as a young man gave his father a Spanish Indian slave; his filial piety was rewarded years later by having bestowed upon him a superior slave. Most men of the time accepted slavery without question — it was in the Bible. In 1687, however, the Massachusetts General Court expressed its disapproval of the kidnapping of slaves, deciding that such slaves should be sent back to " Gynny " with letters of apology and explanation. The difficulties of such a program and the ease of evasion are obvious. In this same year a French traveler noted: " You may also here own Negroes and Negresses. There is not a house in Boston however small may be its means, that has not one or two." Judge Samuel Sewall took a lonely stand against the custom in 1700 by publishing a tract, *The Selling of Joseph.*

Increase Mather lived as his rich and influential associates did. His position was comparable to that of our modern clergymen of importance, with one difference, that he and his fellow ministers of Boston possessed real political power. To them were referred all questions upon which the law was not explicit; and their judgment was final. In those days ministers were statesmen and judges, leaders not only of thought, but of action. The first modern clergyman whose influence was largely through the pulpit was Cotton Mather himself.

Freed of financial worries in 1670 when Cotton was seven, Increase Mather led an ample life. He dined with his friends on the rich diet of the day, heavy in meats and in sweets. Much was the preserving done — damsons, quinces, pears, plums, cherries, barberries, apples, raspberries — much making of cider. Tables groaned under

[11]

heavy helpings of pork, mutton, beef, and all kinds of fish and game. A list of their foods might well make a modern gourmand's mouth water. Twenty-pound lobsters were a reality. Pigeons were so plentiful in Boston as to obscure the sky at times; their numbers were estimated as a million or more; and the townspeople might add squabs to their feasts at two or three pence a dozen. " Wine," wrote Increase Mather in 1673, " is from God," and he and his friends washed down their rich food with plentiful goblets. Potatoes, however, were looked upon askance as a powerful aphrodisiac. As late as 1763 a Hadley farmer's eight-bushel crop was too large, since " if a man ate them every day he could not live beyond seven years." A Parson who had the temerity to raise twenty bushels came near being rebuked by his congregation. A cook-book of 1700 gives a recipe for a dish of potatoes which one can but hope was not followed for those served at Harvard's Commencement dinner of 1708: after being boiled and blanched the potatoes were " seasoned with nutmeg, cinnamon, and pepper, mixed with eringo roots, dates, lemon, and whole mace; covered with butter, sugar, and grape verjuice, made with pastry; then iced with rosewater and sugar."

III

The boy Cotton, then, grew up in a comfortable household where the important men of the colony came to talk and to dine. With wharves at the rear of houses, he saw much of ships. When " a Porpus was pursued and taken within the inward wharfs " small boys gathered to watch the sport; and they watched with interest the arrival and

unloading of ships bringing prominent visitors to their
parents and sweetmeats to them. The Mathers, like their
neighbors, probably raised much of their own food. Not
long before Cotton Mather's birth the president of Harvard College complained to the Corporation " that there
is no ground belonging to the President to keep any cattle
upon; so neither milk, butter, nor cheese, can be had but
by the penny." Prominent Bostonians certainly had food
other than by the penny, for once when Samuel Sewall
was walking with the governor his young son came dash-
ing up to them with the startling news that the cow was
dead. This gave Sewall quite a turn, " understanding him
she had been dead upon a Hill or cast with her Heels
upward, and so had lost Her." This cow which had
served the family well for " above Ten years," dutifully
producing its quota of calves and cream, had now come
to the butcher to be dressed for its last service in the form
of tough roast beef. Sewall also recorded other farm labors,
the making of henhouses, and the felling of trees at
which his womenfolk wept: " Felled the oak at the
E. end of the house. *Matre et Sorore valde plangentibus* "
(Mother and sister copiously weeping). It is then more
than likely that Cotton Mather knew domestic animals
and crops.

Perhaps he even quarreled with his little brothers and
sisters, of whom he had five by the time he was eleven
years old, much as later Sewall's children and his own
did. Sewall's son " Joseph threw a knop of Brass and hit
his Sister Betty on the forehead so as to make it bleed and
swell; upon which, and for his playing at Prayer-time,

and eating when Return Thanks, I whipd him pretty smartly." Cotton Mather's son was punished differently, by seeing his sister given a piece of " pomecitron " while he had none — until she forgivingly shared with him. For Cotton Mather disapproved of corporal punishment: " I would never come, to give a child a *Blow;* except in case of *Obstinacy:* or some gross Enormity."

Cotton Mather himself as a child had his full share of whippings from father and schoolmasters, but he also had his share of citron and raisins, sugared almonds, candy, cider, and beer. Beer was thought good for children, especially warmed. In winter he watched other boys stronger than he sleighing and skating, with the fear of death before him, since many a youth fell through the ice and was drowned. Other boys played the wicked games of football and wicket — as late as 1719 these sports were still so much out of favor that one Boston gentleman turned his grandson out of his house for playing wicket on the Common.

The Boston of Cotton Mather's youth was only a little town of perhaps seven thousand inhabitants cramped into a little peninsula which in high tides was completely cut off from the mainland. Over Boston Neck, when there were no storms to flood it, from the neighboring town crawled ox-carts bearing firewood, charcoal, lumber, salt fish, furs, country produce, and the innumerable wooden articles made in the long cruel winters on farms where wolves howled outside log fences, and great storms kept the population even from Sunday church and Thursday lecture. Over the Bay Path from Springfield and Hadley

The TOWN of
BOSTON
IN
New England
by
Capt. John Bonner
1722

came riders with news of Massachusetts' western frontier; down the coast from Gloucester and Salem sailed the first products of New England shipyards; round the Cape coasted traders manned by bulky Dutchmen from Manhattan; up from the West Indies New England sailors brought molasses and sugar; and now and then sailed into the harbor ships from England with books for the already flourishing Boston bookshops and news of the latest politics at the gay court of his restored Majesty, King Charles II.

Along the narrow streets shops and houses jostled each other. Here was no mystery of commerce and manufacture shut behind forbidding marble façades and grim brick walls. The smell of new wood in carpenters' shops and shipyards, the clangor of the blacksmith's shop, the fresh tarry smell of the rope walks, the acrid odor of tanning pits, the clatter of shoemakers' hammers, the unhappy lowing of beasts waiting to be slaughtered — Boston industry was as close to daily life as the all-pervading smell of the great sea flats at low tide. On Boston Common from time to time some wretch was " turned off the ladder " after urging the quivering crowd to note to what an end Sabbath-breaking and disobedience of parents could bring a man. There were Indians in the streets as there were Indians in the houses and gardens, sullen remnants of conquered Pequots, or " praying Indians " from Natick, or self-possessed emissaries from tribes hunting freely in the wild lands about Brookfield. There was still room in the town for cattle to pasture on the sides of the three hills — as late as 1685 Samuel Sewall wearied

[15]

himself " in walking from one end and side of the Town
to t'other to seak [his] loſt Cow."

IV

Fortunate indeed was Cotton Mather that to him reading was the greateſt of delights. In his father's book-lined
ſtudy he learned before he could read that love of books
for which he was always noted. Perhaps he received permission to come home from Harvard in 1676, when, two
days after the great fire that deſtroyed his father's church
and house, the family bent their energies to drying the
books which, chief of their possessions, had been saved.
Cotton Mather was the son and grandson of authors;
books on his father's shelves bore the names of John Cotton, of Richard Mather, and of Increase Mather himself.
Certainly the *Bay Psalm Book,* of which Richard Mather
was part author, had its place there — that pious but
halting verse version of the Psalms of which the authors
said: ". . . wee have respeﬆed rather a plaine transla-
tion, then to smooth our verses with the sweetnes of any
paraphrase, and soe have attended Conscience rather than
Elegance, fidelity rather then poetry, in translating the
hebrew words into english language, and Davids poetry
into English meetre; that soe we may sing in Sion the
Lords songs of prayse according to his owne will." John
Cotton spoke particularly of its virtue in being closer to
the original and free from " divers other defeﬆs (which
we cover in silence) " of the version hitherto in use. But
all the books in this library were not pious, though there
were traﬆs, sermons, and church hiſtories in abundance.

[16]

There were also almanacks, medical books, secular histories, the *Body of Chymiſtry,* travel books, Herbert's poems, and more than a five-foot shelf of classics in Greek and Latin, including Æsop and Plautus, and even Ovid's *Art of Love.* Here was amusement enough for any ſtudious boy.

Cotton Mather was more than usually ſtudious, but he was no special prodigy of holiness in spite of the faɕt that holy children were fairly common. In an age which moſt valued piety children soon learned that one way to attraɕt attention was to get religion. " Anne Greenough . . . left the world when she was but about five years old, and yet gave aſtonishing discoveries of a regard unto God and Chriſt, and her own soul, before she went away." She " had an unspeakable delight in catechising. . . . She was very frequent and conſtant in secret prayer, and could not with any patience be interrupted in it. When she fell sick . . . she would not . . . be diverted from the thoughts of death, wherein she took such pleasure, that she did not care to hear any thing else. And if she were asked, ' whether she were willing to die? ' she would ſtill cheerfully reply, ' Ay, by all means, that I may go to the Lord Jesus Chriſt'! "

Cotton Mather's younger brother Nathaniel was a holy child who managed to grow in piety until he was nineteen. Four years younger than Cotton, he sought God even more earneſtly. At fourteen he entered " into covenant with God " and drew up a liſt of Scriptural references for the regulation of his affeɕtions, his speech, and his work. At night he would ask himself:

[17]

" I What has God's Mercy been with me this day?
II What has my carriage to God been this day?
III If I die this night, is my immortal spirit safe? "

One of Cotton Mather's own daughters died at the age of two and a half, a devout Christian, loving Christ passionately.

But it was not until he was fourteen that Cotton Mather himself began his days of secret prayer and fasting; and he was eight or nine before he even began to exhort his schoolfellows to piety, receiving for reward a just meed of blows. For there were ordinary boys even then who preferred forbidden play to secret prayer. Nevertheless, where modern education begins with play, Puritan education began with pray. A child as soon as it could speak was taught to answer catechisms and to address the Deity, imploring a chance to escape damnation. The laws of the stern Judge who sentenced to hell all but the most carefully chosen must be minutely observed; direct acquaintance with these laws was imperative for the least hope of salvation. The sooner a child learned to read the sooner he could have direct acquaintance with the bulwark of the civilization into which he was born; that bulwark was the Bible. What other reason for learning to read?

As early as 1647 the Massachusetts General Court had promulgated this order: " It being one cheefe piect of that ould deluder, Satan, to keepe men from the knowledge of the Scriptures, as in former times by keeping them in an unknown tongue, so in these latter times by pswading from the use of tongues, that so at least the true sence &

meaning of the originall might be clouded by false glosses of saint seeming deceivers, that learning may not be buried in the grave of our fathers in the church & commonwealth the Lord assisting our endeavours, —

" It is therefore ordered, that every township in this iurisdiction after the Lord hath increased them to the number of 50 householders, shall then forthwith appoint one within their towne to teach all such children as shall resort to him to write & reade."

Cotton Mather was an afflicted child — he stuttered badly — had need to begin early to climb the path to the Bible. In 1691 Judge Sewall wrote in his diary: " This afternoon had Joseph to school to Capt. Townsend's Mother's, his Cousin Jane accompanying him, carried his Horn-book." At this time Joseph lacked four months of being three years old. As the colony grew older, the children were not more, but less, precocious. It is therefore more than likely that Cotton Mather was either taught at home or sent to a dame school soon after he was two. At such schools little children learned to read, starting with the hornbooks which could conveniently be tied to their sides — thus serving the double purpose of handy instruction and constant impediment to activity. A hornbook was a tablet of wood over which was placed a sheet of paper with the alphabet, a group of simple syllables, and the Lord's Prayer. Over the paper was a protecting sheet of transparent horn of yellowish hue. Books for children who had successfully passed through the syllabic stage of the hornbook were invariably pious. There were easy rhymes — as simple in their diction as in their be-good-and-you-will-be-happy morality — and pleasant tales of the conversion of children and of the lives of children " in whom the love of God was remarkable Budding before they died," with romance brought in through the lives of bad children who after delightfully detailed naughtinesses repented and were saved, or didn't repent and were damned. John Cotton's *Spiritual Milk for Boston Babes* which was *Drawn from the Breasts of Both Testaments* was taken first in sips and then in gulps by his precocious grandson, who himself later wrote books for children embodying the idea of them both, that a child by well-directed lessons could grow in piety as it grew in learning.

Earlier than most boys, Cotton Mather passed into " the free school in Boston," where he was taught by two learned men, the second the famous schoolmaster Ezekiel Cheever, who rejoiced in this student who required no beatings for inattention. He absorbed the lessons of the masters, but failed to comprehend those of his worldly schoolfellows. His frail health gave excuse for protection against their tyranny; and he was presumably housebound during the severe weeks of the winter. Instead of taking his chances in snowball fights, the boy curled up in a deep chair before the fire in his father's library. His mother was busy managing servants and bearing babies; his father hurried about on affairs of church and state, sometimes taking long journeys. Once Increase Mather took the long trail to Northampton to guide his dying brother's steps to eternity; and falling ill himself was detained for months. When he was home he spent hours with his books,

reading, writing, and guiding the education of his precocious son. These were happy days for the boy, when,
safe from the rude attacks of less studious youngsters, safe
even from the importunities of the household's numerous
babies, he and his father read and talked. His avidity for
knowledge led him far beyond the requirements of school;
he did not " do lessons "; he read and absorbed, and read
again. When visitors came he would let his book fall and
listen intently to the conversation, whether of church or
state, gaining an ever-increasing admiration for this father
of his who could with equal assurance guide a lad in his
studies and great men in their lives and activities. It was
his father — together, of course, with other ministers
almost as wise and as powerful as he — who actually
guided the state. Right here in his father's study the government of the colony was discussed and settled; for he
soon saw that what the ministers decided happened. It
was, he thought, almost like being the son of a king.

His father talked with God, too. At one time the holy
child Nathaniel was very ill; Increase Mather decreed for
himself a day of prayer and humiliation as a means of
saving the boy's life, permitting the young Cotton to share
this solemn occasion with him. It was a favor he rapidly
regretted, for at the close of the day he wrote in his diary:
" Now I thought it might be some discouragement to
Cotton in case Hee shd see that his poor sinfull Fathers
prayrs were not heard; tho I humbly pleaded with God."
But his prayers were heard, Nathaniel was saved, and
Cotton at twelve could leave home for Cambridge confident of his father's favor at the heavenly court.

[21]

CHAPTER TWO

"The *slavish* way of *Education* carried on with
raving and kicking and scourging (in *Schools* as
well as *Families*,) tis abominable."
— *The Diary of Cotton Mather*

I

CAMBRIDGE was a fair journey by horseback
and ferry. Thither at twelve with a reading
and speaking knowledge of Latin, a reading
knowledge of Greek, and some knowledge of Hebrew,
came Cotton Mather, an infant prodigy for Harvard. At
this time his father cherished the hope of the college presidency, then vacant, with Urian Oakes acting president.
On a visit to Cambridge, Increase Mather discussed the
matter with Oakes, saying that he was falsely reported to
covet the office. Oakes soothingly replied that everyone
knew that Increase could have the presidency at any time
would he but accept of it, but there had been fear expressed
that he (Increase) would try to remove the college to
Boston. He was sure, however, that this fear was unwar-
ranted and that he should yet see Increase presiding in
Cambridge. But it was not until long after his brilliant
young son's graduation that Increase Mather finally
realized his ambition.

It was in 1675 that the boy entered Harvard. That
summer he heard the drums beating for volunteers and
saw the militia, with old armor polished and old match-

locks furbished, marching off to help put down Sagamore Philip and his allied Indians. It was clear from the start that this was no insignificant uprising. When the news of massacres, burnings, captivities, ambushes, and skirmishings began to drift into Boston, when tribe after tribe rose against the settlers in all parts of the Commonwealth, it was apparent that Massachusetts was fighting for its life.

The causes were simple enough. The Indians were nomadic hunters with a rudimentary agriculture, still in the Stone Age culture; the colonists were settled agriculturists. Constantly the colonists pressed upon the Indians, inclosing their hunting-grounds until there was literally no place for them to go. Moreover, the colonists regarded the Indians with ill-disguised contempt. Thirty years before they had exterminated the Pequots in Connecticut, since when they had had no great regard for the Indian as a fighter. They had learned the Indians' weaknesses and knew that in the end — though the struggle be hard — there could be no question which race would be victorious. Moreover, they regarded the Indians literally as children of the devil, capable of doing harm with magical ceremonies. Indians had no recognizable rights unless they embraced Christianity, adopted European ways, and conformed to colonial laws and sovereignty. It was a situation intolerable to both sides.

The people of Boston speedily envisaged the Indians as perpetrators of inhuman outrages; and a fully developed series of atrocities immediately appeared, zealously fanned by the population who took no actual part in the fighting.

[23]

To the boy Cotton Mather the war was explained as one more of the devil's attacks upon God's people, and he stored in his mind enough of the vituperation and hatred of the "bloody savages" to furnish forth a vivid chapter in his *Magnalia* twenty years later. The Indians were perfidious, barbarous, murderous, blasphemous, surly, haughty, insolent; they were cruel tawnies, beasts of prey, devils in flesh, savages of prodigious barbarity, rabid animals; Philip was a bloody and crafty wretch with a venomous and murderous heart. The colonists were an honest, harmless, Christian generation of English; the colonial soldiers were valiant and prudent.

The atrocities were, of course, blood-curdling. There were mangled bodies with their heads stuck on poles, and Bibles torn to pieces in defiance of holy religion. Five or six of the imprisoned colonists were forced to run a gauntlet and were barbarously whipped; hot ashes were thrown on them; collops of their living flesh were cut and the wounds cauterized; and thus " with exquisite, leisurely, horrible torments," they were " roasted . . . out of the world."

It is clear what the twelve-year-old Boston boy heard of the fighting in Massachusetts woods from refugees, soldiers, and spreaders of rumor. His elders showed all the hatred that comes from a thoroughly roused fear. Cotton Mather saw the friendly Christianized Indians of Natick hounded out of their pleasant homes by a frenzied populace bent on wreaking vengeance on the innocent, since the guilty were beyond their reach. He saw the

Indians with their sick and lame set on board boats and
shipped to bleak, shelterless Deer Island in the Bay,
" patiently, humbly, and piously," says Eliot, the gentle
apostle, " without murmuring or complaining against the
English," shaming in their Christian spirit the Christianity of those who had divine assurance of salvation. He
saw the wretched Indian women and children whom
Philip had been forced to abandon herded into Boston as
prisoners of war, farmed out as slaves for a while in the
town, and at last, including Philip's wife and son, shipped
off as slaves to the murderous sugar plantations of the
West Indies. His father, Increase Mather, as one of the
ministers to whom the fate of the captives was referred,
had urged that an " effectual course " be taken with King
Philip's son. Increase Mather was all for severe action
against the Indians. There was in the Mather family little
sympathy for Eliot's saintly plea: " The humble petition
of John Eliot showeth that the terror of selling away such
Indians into the Islands for perpetual slavery, who shall
yield themselves to your mercy, is like to be an effectual
prolongation of the war. . . . Christ hath said: ' Blessed
are the merciful, for they shall obtain mercy.' This usage
of them is worse than death. . . . My humble request
is that you would follow Christ his designs in this matter
to foster the passages of religion among them, and not to
destroy them. . . ." When the enemies of God's kingdom in Massachusetts were in the power of the Commonwealth, this was a language which Increase Mather
did not understand.

King Philip's war continued for a year with massacres

and battles, outrages and pillagings, ending at laſt with the death of Philip, trapped in his native country. " He fell upon his face in the mud and water, with his gun under him. . . . Captain Church ordered his body to be pulled out of the mire to the upland. So some of Captain Church's Indians took hold of him by his ſtockings, and by his small breeches (being otherwise naked) and drew him through the mud to the upland; and a doleful, great, naked, dirty beaſt he looked like. Captain Church then said, that foreasmuch as he had caused many an Englishman's body to be unburied, and to rot above ground, that not one of his bones should be buried. And calling his old Indian executioner, bid him behead and quarter him. . . . And so he went to work and did as he was ordered."

The war ended forever the power of the southern New England Indians. Henceforth they were a broken and subjeƈt race, unable by themselves to infliƈt more than occasional damage to the coloniſts. But the memory of the war remained vivid. It had coſt Massachusetts the destruƈtion or abandonment of sixteen towns, the loss of one-sixteenth of her men of military age, and the expenditure of thousands of pounds. It had, however, given the coloniſts a feeling of independence; without the help of the home country they had wreſted final control of the new land from their enemies.

This, then, was the background for Cotton Mather's entrance at Harvard, America's firſt ſtate college brought into being by an aƈt of legislature in the firſt decade of the colony's founding. To the meager appropriations from the State treasury had been added contributions of books, money, land, and salt cellars from public-minded citizens.

II

Intellectually, Boston boys were not spared, though physically their lot was far removed from that of the children of Plymouth, who were obliged to work early, long, and hard to help their parents tear a living out of the soil. These overworked lads of Plymouth, in order to get the " raines off their necks," sometimes ran away, some becoming " souldiers, others took upon them for long viages by sea, and others some worse course tending to dissoluteness and the dangers of their soules." But this handful of Boston boys deStined to be the leaders of the colony, though theirs were homes of plenty, were none the less driven. To enter Harvard these boys were obliged to " underStand *Tully,* or such like classicall Latine Author *extempore,* and make and speake true Latine in Verse and Prose . . . ; And decline perfectly the Paradigim's of *Nounes* and *Verbes* in the *Greek* tongue."

Once admitted, these lads found their hours fairly well charted from seven in the morning, when the day opened with Scripture and prayer, from which, however, one " cut " a week was even thus early permissible: " But if any (without necessary impediment) shall absent himself from prayer or Lectures, he shall be lyable to Admonition, if he offend above once a weeke." The heavy grind of Arithmetick and Geometry, with a dash of AStronomy at the close, Logick, Physicks, Ethicks, and Politicks,

[27]

Greeke, Hebrew, Chaldee, and Syriack, was varied by constant Declamations.

" Every Schollar that on proofe is found able to read the Originalls of the *Old* and *New Testament* into the Latine tongue, and to resolve them *Logically;* withall being of godly life and conversation; And at any publick Act hath the Approbation of the Overseers and Master of the Colledge, is fit to be dignified with his first Degree.

" Every Schollar that giveth up in writing a *System,* or *Synopsis,* or summe of *Logick,* Naturall and Morall *Phylosophy, Arithmetick, Geometry* and *Astronomy:* and is ready to defend his *Theses* or positions: withall skilled in the Originalls as abovesaid: and of godly life & conversation: and so approved by the Overseers and Master of the Colledge, at any publique *Act,* is fit to be dignified with his 2d. Degree."

The original seminary, housed in a building shut in by a fence six and a half feet high, had gathered nine boys who suffered under the stern discipline of a man soon dismissed for beating an usher, " a gentleman born," for " the space of two hours " with " a cudgel big enough to have killed a horse, and a yard in length." The seminary had rapidly turned into a college with a president, a corporation, and a group of overseers. All it lacked was a body of loyal and critical alumni and these time had furnished by the time Cotton entered, himself the son of an alumnus. He found himself one of a group of twelve boys religious and church-tamed, but none, not even his own cousin John Cotton, quite so free from

EARLIEST PRINT OF HARVARD COLLEGE, 1726

worldly taint as this youngest lad fresh from a home where God spoke constantly to one and all. These boys had to be forbidden " dice, cards, and other species of gaming for money." They were not to buy or sell anything beyond the value of sixpence without the consent of their parents. They were to be whipped — not exceeding ten stripes for each offense. They had also to be forbidden " to force a freshman or junior to go on errands or do other services, by blows, threats, or language of any kind." If physical prowess accompanied mental vigor, the precocious child's lot would have been happier then and now. But the bookworm is seldom muscular and the praise of his teachers counts with his classmates only as an excuse for physical torture. He who beats his elders in the classroom is beaten by them in the yard. Cotton Mather, coming to his father's college full of learning and godliness, stammering the more from excitement, was at a disadvantage among older boys who knew less of books and more of life than he. He came to college much like the modern freshman, filled with high and noble ideals, prepared to be humble in the presence of faculty and seniors, people more learned than he. Like the modern youth, he meant to watch his manners and his language lest he appear uncouth in the eyes of his more finished associates. And — still like the modern youth — he saw his ideals crash at the first impact. Here was no group of earnest boys nobly striving to keep covenant with God and the corporation; here was no republic of intellectual striving and high moralizing. Sheltered as he had been, he did not know that boys remained barbarians even when they went to college, even when they were preparing for the ministry. Here they were away from home and parental authority, with money in their pockets and unsupervised time on their hands. Rules? Of course there were rules. But did the lad think juniors and seniors kept rules? One did as one chose, and one didn't get found out.

Cotton Mather at twelve was innocent and credulous; he was fair sport. Since his natural tendency was obedience, he must be made to break rules; and slyly, so that to his horror over his disobedience would be added the horror of escaping the penalty. These dozen lads put their heads together and laid traps for the boy. They would use their most daring curses casually in his presence; they would force him to watch their card games and make him run to the store for a fresh pack of cards, which he carried as if they were indeed the devil's instruments he thought them; they would make him lend them his few pennies to stake on the game. By cunningly devised questions they would trick him into what seemed to him blasphemous statements. They would snatch his books and send him on foolish errands. They laughed at him, teased him, kept him from his studies, and tortured him in every way known to tough-skinned youth. The sensitive boy suffered out of all proportion; he saw his whole world arrayed against him. The persecution mania that had threatened him in his school days now fastened itself firmly upon him, to distort his views for all time. At home he had been treated with respect; his father encouraged him, his mother stood in awe of his learning; his brothers and sisters had early been trained not to disturb him at his books. He had come to regard himself and his pursuit of knowledge with seriousness. But these rude boys — who, he had thought, would be his companions at the table of knowledge — gave him not respect, but ridicule. He could have stood their profanity and their lawlessness; he could not stand their ridicule. Throughout his life, whether his neighbors' mirth was kindly or malicious, he saw in it only persecution. Thus Harvard wove one more heavy strand to a disposition already weighted with piety, filial duty, and fear of sudden death.

It was natural for the boy to refer his trouble to his father. Increase Mather paused in his numerous tasks to seek a way out for his boy; he noted in his diary that when he studied to write his sermons he was " much hindered by Trouble at Cottons being abused by John Cotton, & some other scholars at the college." So much hindered was he that he saw no way out but to ride to Cambridge and himself talk to the misguided " scholars." He had an especially serious talk with his wife's nephew, John Cotton, whom he regarded as the ringleader of his boy's tormentors. John Cotton readily agreed that it was not good for the reputation of Harvard to have freshmen used as errand boys; he knew enough not to dispute with an alumnus worried about the tone of his college. Having given his uncle assurance for future goodwill toward his cousin, he waved him a genial farewell and went off to join his fellows in planning some new sport with the infant prodigy — in case he should think his father's interference could protect him. And now there were no further appeals to the students; the president himself should hear of this. Forthwith Increase Mather bestrode his horse and arrived at Cambridge, hot and indignant. Oakes, the acting president, found it wise to summon one of the fellows to help him soothe this wrathful alumnus and persuade him not to remove his son. They praised the boy's intellect, they pointed out his necessity for just the kind of training Harvard would give him, they reasoned that he would soon learn to adjust himself to the other boys, and would in turn initiate other freshmen. They played upon the elder Mather's love of his son and love of his Alma Mater; and he finally left for home outwardly mollified. And he kept Cotton at Harvard, though, as he reflected on the interview, he more than suspected that he had been hoodwinked: " Rode to Cambridge where discoursd with mr danforth & Mr Okes about taking Cotton from Colledge and they were loth that I should do it yet could not give satisfactory answere to my Reasons."

The boy remained; and in time his sufferings lessened. Yet he cherished for his classmates no such affection as his friend Samuel Sewall kept to the end of his life: " Now I can go to no more Funerals of my Classmates; nor none be at mine, for the survivers, the Rev'd Mr. Samuel Mather at Windsor, and the Revᵈ Mr. Taylor at Westfield are one Hundred Miles off, and are entirely enfeebled."

III

Cotton Mather's immediate classmates were three: his cousin John Cotton, who became a preacher, dying in time

to leave a widow to become the second wife of Cotton
Mather's father; Urian Oakes, the consumptive son of the
college president; and Grindall Rawson, son of the secretary of Massachusetts Colony and descendant of the sister
of Queen Elizabeth's Archbishop of Canterbury, himself
later becoming the strictest of clergymen. In the class
above Cotton Mather there were six boys, three of whom
were the sons of ministers, one the son of a captain, and
one the son of a weaver. Four of these six boys became
ministers. One of them, Thomas, the son of the famous
and by no means gentle schoolmaster, Ezekiel Cheever,
later had trouble with his church, being dismissed for
" Great Scandals." Of the three seniors two became ministers, one of them being the son of that Reverend Thomas
Shepard whose terrible depictings of hell fed his parishioners' appetites for horror. This son of his " would
not only on the *Lord's Days,* while he was yet a boy, so
notably repeat *by heart* in his Father's Family, all the
Heads of the Longest Sermons preached in the Publick,
that it might have served for a sufficient Repetition, instead of using the Notes usually produced on such Occasions." Beyond doubt he inherited his father's love of
horrors with which a lad like Cotton Mather might be
regaled. The other future minister was the son of a wheel-
wright. This young man was older than the others in
college, being twenty-one when twelve-year-old Cotton
Mather entered. The third member of this class was that
same Thomas Brattle who became a veritable thorn in
the flesh to Increase and Cotton Mather. His liberal religious views, which later gained him the epithets of

[33]

"apostate" and "infidel," were already sufficiently pronounced to antagonize the youthful prodigy. Brattle had leanings toward the Episcopal Church. Shocking indeed must his sentiments have seemed to the young Cotton Mather. Moreover, Brattle even thus early evinced that calm judicial mind which could see beyond the prejudice and hysteria of the moment, though he was never one to martyr himself for his opinions. He it was who, as treasurer of Harvard, later helped along the opposition to Cotton Mather's father, the "reverend scribbler" who turned about to call Brattle a "moral heathen." The church whose founding caused the Mathers such agony was of his making; it bore his name and he chose its pastor. And in 1692, after the excitement had begun to subside, he opposed the already declining persecution of witches which seemed to Cotton Mather the only way to defend God and drive out the devil. Hence it is hardly likely that Thomas Brattle and Cotton Mather could have been congenial spirits at Harvard.

Of the four boys who entered the year after Cotton Mather, one was the sickly son of the deputy-governor and one the son of the college president. Both these boys died young. The third became a worthy minister, dying at thirty-nine; and the fourth another learned minister who survived somewhat longer. None of these became important.

But in the following class of five boys, entering the year before Cotton Mather graduated, were two boys a year older than he who were to become the objects of his bitter enmity. One, John Leverett, was chosen president of Harvard at a time when Cotton Mather longed for the honor himself. The other boy was William, brother of the Thomas Brattle who had graduated two years before. As he shared his brother's liberal religious views, he, too, became anathema to the Mathers.

In college, then, Cotton Mather was bred among his future enemies. It is therefore curiously ironical that his father thought it necessary to ask the president to protect him. Doubtless Cotton, too, felt called upon to defend his father, for Increase Mather at this time was certain that he was ill-spoken of at the college. He went to Oakes, saying that he knew that the scholars told untrue tales of him; he felt that they had been permitted to do so. Whether or not his son Cotton was his informant he did not state; but he was determined to resign his office as Fellow with all due wrath. He told Oakes he was not " willing to continue as Fellow any longer, because I had bin so abused in Cambridge." He went to the governor with his tale and the governor said, " it was not to be suffered." Nevertheless, Oakes managed to soothe his ire and he remained a Fellow and his son Cotton a student, doubtless less popular than ever for telling tales.

Just before Cotton Mather's entrance into Harvard a student had been disciplined for " speaking blasphemous words concerning the H. G.," being " publickly whipped before all the scholars " by an " instrument " wielded by Goodman Hely before whom the culprit kneeled. This boy's degree was withheld, and he was further required to " sit alone by himself in the Hall uncovered at meals."

It is to be hoped that these meals were better than those

served Cotton Mather's uncle and his mates when the college was young. Then the principal's lady, when her husband was questioned " about the ill and scant diet of his boarders, (for, though their friends gave large allowance, yet their diet was ordinarily nothing but porridge and pudding, and that very homely,)" admitted her sin in denying them beef and cheese when both were in the house and in serving them breakfast neither " well boiled or stirred "; bad fish, too, she had been guilty of serving them. " And for their mackerel, brought to them with their guts in them, and goats' dung in their hasty pudding, it's utterly unknown to me; but I am much ashamed it should be in the family, and not prevented by myself or servants, and I humbly acknowledge my negligence in it. And that they made their beds at any time, were my straits never so great, I am sorry they were ever put to it."

In 1680, before Cotton had taken his second degree, a Dutch scholar described Harvard thus: " Cambridge . . . is not a large village and the houses stand very much apart. The college building is the most conspicuous among them. We went to it, expecting to see something unusual, as it is the only college, or would-be academy of the Protestants in all America, but we found ourselves mistaken. In approaching the house we neither heard nor saw anything mentionable; but going to the other side of the building, we heard noise enough in an upper room to lead my comrade to say, ' I believe they are engaged in disputation.' We entered and went upstairs. . . . We found there eight or ten young fellows sitting around,

smoking tobacco with the smoke of which the room was
so full, that you could hardly see; and the whole house
smelt so ſtrong of it that when I was going upſtairs I
said, ' It muſt certainly be also a tavern.' We excused ourselves, that we could speak English only a little. . . .
However, we spoke as well as we could. We inquired how
many professors there were, and they replied not one,
that there was not enough money to support one. We
asked how many ſtudents there were. They said at firſt,
thirty, and then came down to twenty; I afterwards underſtood there are probably not ten. [Aĉtually there were
juſt thirty, of whom about half, including Cotton Mather,
were graduate ſtudents.] They knew hardly a word of
Latin, not one of them, so that my comrade could not
converse with them." This, however, was the view of a
prejudiced visitor. As a matter of faĉt, a speaking knowledge of Latin was required for admittance; and among
the nineteen rules of the college, rules which ſtarted with
requirements of admission and passed through regulations of conduĉt, thought, and ſtudy, the second being,
" Every one shall consider the main end of his life and
ſtudies, to know God and Jesus Chriſt, which is eternal
life; John xvii. 3 "; and the ninth, " None shall prag-
matically intrude or intermeddle in other men's affairs ";
among these rules the thirteenth was: " The scholars shall
never use their mother tongue, except that in public exercises of oratory, or such like, they be called to make
them in English." In later years when his own son had
juſt graduated, Cotton Mather himself, now a prominent
alumnus, a *laudator temporis aĉti,* among other sugges-

tions to a committee of investigation wrote: " Whether the speaking of Latin has not been so discountenanced as to render our scholars very unfit for a conversation with strangers "; which presumably was not the case in the good old days when he was a student.

It is certain that the fifteen-year-old boy who at the end of the usual three-year course came up for his B.A. in 1678 understood the Latin eloquence of the president; it is to be hoped that the fellow students who had tortured him also understood the weighty praise: ". . . Cotton Mather . . . What a Name! I beg pardon, Gentlemen, I should have said, what Names! I shall say nothing of the Minister, his Father, a most diligent Member of the Corporation, one of the foremost fellows of our municipal College; I ought not to praise him publickly in his presence; but if he brings back and represents the Piety, the Erudition, the elegant Ability, the Sound Sense, the Prudence, and the Dignity of his GRANDFATHERS the most reverend JOHN COTTON and RICHARD MATHER, he may be said to have gained success; nor do I lack hope but that in this youth COTTON and MATHER in fact as well as in name will unite and live again." Here was balm for his hurts. What sensitive brilliant boy, however, could fail to be awed into a feeling of unworthiness and led into a straining of all his powers by such a conclusion?

IV

It was in the next year that he joined the church after deep searching of his soul. For this was no easy religion; the rewards it had to offer both here and hereafter were too great for the multitude. Only the chosen could enjoy God's favor on earth and in heaven; and only one thing was certain — that one's chance to be chosen was naught unless one entered the church, membership in which was dependent on a public profession of faith.

Church membership was essential not only to heavenly but to earthly election, since suffrage was the privilege of church members alone. Every one, to be sure, was compelled to attend church services; church membership, however, was a privilege. Upon entering the church with a public confession of faith one took out citizenship papers for heaven and for Massachusetts.

Candidacy for preferment, temporal and eternal, was announced in advance, that a full congregation might attend to hear the pledge of allegiance to God's banner in New England. There may have been men of callous courage able to go through this ordeal with tongue in cheek, seeking only the earthly gain of the vote. Certainly the sixteen-year-old Cotton Mather could not face a large gathering of Boston's leading citizens flanked by the common herd, come to see the show, Brahmin and sinner alike alert to criticize, without feeling the full weight of his heritage of Cotton and Mather piety. At Harvard Commencement he had been watched for his learning; and there he had had companions whose illustrious ancestry had also been praised. Now he stood alone, and upon him rested the burden of the faith of his faithful fathers. Sensitive, near-sighted, studious, slender of body, a late adolescent, from his slow physical development he had gained religious fervor. The moral and religious

[39]

craving of adolescents which serves to divert their minds from the bodily changes was especially strong in this mentally precocious lad whose highest ambition — to enter the calling of his fathers — seemed permanently thwarted. His stutter, persisting in spite of the numerous prayers poured forth by his parents and himself, forbade his entering the ministry. The failure of the Lord to answer these prayers might, indeed, indicate that to him the gates of heavenly preferment were also closed.

He looked at his father's friends and tried desperately to control his tongue, to make it utter the words which would prove him worthy to sit among them even though he could not lead them from the pulpit. It was his first chance to preach — and probably his last. His stammering speech made difficult the expression of the visions his delayed adolescence had vivified, the glory of God that had seared his soul. He was only sixteen; he felt that unless he could draw near to the Presence he could not breathe; he must touch the mantle of the Lord; he must feel that he was guided from above; he must feel that he was worth being given a chance of salvation. And though his tongue stumbled, he did not disgrace his ancestry.

v

Even so no swift miracle improved his impediment. He and his father prayed and considered; and finally decided that since he could not tend men's souls, he would tend their bodies.

At this time medicine had far to go. Men were credulous in this as in all scientific fields. Mermaids and mermen were accredited facts. A sailor on the boat that in 1686 brought the bookseller Dunton to Boston had seen both on voyages to the East Indies. " And the Neitherland History tells us of a Meermaid that was taken there, that was both Taught to spin, and perform several other petty offices of Women. . . . And . . . in the year 1576, there was taken in Norway a certain Fish resembling a Mitred Bishop." Dunton believed this; and yet he was a man of education and good sense; a man who could reflect that " A Fool and a Wise Man are both alike in the Starting-place, their Birth; and at the Post, their death. Only they differ in the race of their Lives; And this begat in me another reflection, which is, That one may get Wisdom by looking on a Fool."

At this time, too, monstrous births were realities, the result of bestiality or of religious infidelity. Examples of the latter were furnished by Anne Hutchinson and by " one very nearly related unto this gentlewoman, and infected with her heresies." Anne Hutchinson, that " *erroneous gentlewoman* herself, convicted of holding about *thirty* monstrous opinions, growing big with child, and at length coming to her time of travail, was delivered of about *thirty* monstrous births at once; whereof some were bigger, some were lesser; of several figures; few of any perfect, none of any *humane* shape." These however might be but physical misconceptions corresponding to the poor lady's religious misconceptions. But her relative had been " delivered of as hideous a *monster* as perhaps the sun ever lookt upon. It had no head; the face was below the breast: the ears were like an ape's, and grew upon the shoulders; the eyes and mouth stood far out; the nose was hooking upwards; the breast and back were full of short prickles, like a thorn-back; the navel, belly, and the distinction of sex, which was female, were in the place of the hips; and those back-parts were on the same side with the face; the arms, hands, thighs and legs, were as other childrens; but instead of toes, it had on each foot three claws, with talons like a fowl: upon the back above the belly it had a couple of great holes like mouths; and in each of them stood out a couple of pieces of flesh; it had no forehead, but above the eyes it had four horns; two of above an inch long, hard and sharp; and the other two somewhat less." This description is incorporated in Cotton Mather's most serious work, which further states that a few days afterwards because of rumor " the magistrates ordered the opening of the grave, whereby there was discovered this *Monstrum, horrendum, informe, ingens.*"

Deformities were ascribed to witchcraft. Cotton Mather's own first son, born in 1693, lacked an anus, and in spite of efforts to relieve him, died in three days. Mather more than suspected witchcraft, his wife having been frightened some few weeks before by a *Spectre;* furthermore, a tormented young woman told how the spectres boasted that they had caused this mischief; and finally a woman suspected of unholy dealings had written a letter reviling Cotton Mather to his father Increase, saying, *" Hee little knew what might quickly befall some of his posterity."*

It is not, then, surprising that medical treatment —

when not surgical and fatal — was half magical. Medical knowledge was dependent upon books which were like to include recipes for remedies and sometimes for good food since one authority asserted that no one could be a good doctor who was not also well acquainted with cookery. Here is the germ of those portly volumes in country homes and seaside cottages from which one may still learn how to make chowders, pickle onions, stir up poultices, and dose the sick.

Occasionally there were autopsies when the relatives of those who died wondrous deaths were reasonable. The ills of the times were in themselves remarkable. People then had a fine habit of vomiting up worms — due, doubtless, to the diseased pork and beef they ate — and bewitched children, even more skillful in vomit, produced pins and nails of great length. The Boston *Weekly News Letter* of January 14, 1717, however, records the most striking case: " One Thomas Smith a Sawyer about four Months ago, bought a Lusty Tall new negro, fit for his Employ, who after complain'd of something within him that made a Noise Chip, Chip, Chip; his Master sent for a Doctor, one Sebastian Henry Swetzet, a German, who told him he had Worms, whereupon he gave him some Physick on Wednesday: from Thursday till the Lords Day he gave him some Powders, which on the Lords Day had that effect as to cause him to vomit up a long Worm, that measur'd a hundred and twenty eight Foot, which the negro took to be his Guts; it was almost as big as ones little Finger, its Head was like a Snakes, and would receive a Mans little Finger into its Mouth, it was of a whitish Colour all full of Joynts, its tail was long and hard, and with a Microscope it seem'd to be hairy; the Negro before voiding the Worm had an extraordinary Stomach." Unwilling to believe in this worm on mere hearsay, Cotton Mather, no longer a medical student, requested John Perkins, his physician, to investigate the matter. Perkins reported to Mather that although the neighbors had taken away pieces of the worm as souvenirs, he found remaining one hundred and twenty-eight feet. He thought the worm similar to that described in a publication of the Royal Society to which Mather now sent an account of this American parallel.

To cope with such ills and others — smallpox, measles, violent " feavours," gout, headaches — medicine had to be as powerful as the diseases. There was a limit to the amount of blood that could be taken from a patient, but there was no limit to the imagination of the medicine-mixers. The two schools of medicine — the " chymical," relying on metals, and the natural, relying on herbs — were reconciled in America, doctors cheerfully trying both. Jewels and gold were, however, too scarce to figure largely in the colonists' pharmacopœia; and it is altogether possible that Cotton Mather never swallowed a single pearl or leaf of gold in his sickness-beset life. Antimony and coral were less costly and may have helped along his sufferings. In 1682 Governor John Winthrop, who dosed many a Connecticut Puritan, lamented, " I am straitened, having no ivory beaten, neither any pearle nor coral." Doubtless he also lacked rubies, amber, and " amber-griese." Others with less regal tastes inclined to herbs —

[44]

alehoof, garlic, elder, sage, rue, saffron, and many another plant carefully brought from England to become the weeds of the new country; and leaned heavily on sowbugs or millepedes, those flat horrors that lurk under sodden logs. A pleasant remedy was Aqua Magnanimitatis, which stirred up courage and increased magnanimity — " It doth also wonderfully wake up those any way slothful ": " Take of Ants or Pismires a handful, of their Eggs two hundred, of Millipedes, i.e., Woodlice, one hundred, of honey Bees one hundred and fifty: digest these in two pints of spirits of Wine, being very well impregnated with the brightest soot; digest them together for the space of a month, then pour off the mother tincture and keep it safe. This must be dilute with water or spirit." Other recipes equally delightful are found in this medical book published in 1657: The Magestry of Blood; Elixir of Mummy; The Essence of Man's-brains; A famous Spirit of Cranium; the Bears-balsam; the Quintessance of Snakes, Adders, and Vipers; The Water of the Sperm of Frogs. Fortunately for the sick, these medicines, though they were infallible for falling-sickness, fits, or the stag-gers, as well as for " all inward inflammations," were recommended in very small doses. Sometimes so powerful were they that " a scruple, or a drop or two, . . . in some specifical water once a day," was sufficient. Such was The Essence of Man's-brains: " Take the Brains of a young man, that hath died a violent death, togeather with its membranes, Arteries, Veins, Nerves, and all the pith of the Back bone; bruise these in a stone mortar till they become a kind of pap, then putt as much of the Spirits

[45]

of Vine as will cover three or four fingers bredth; then put it into a large glass, that three parts of four be empty, being Hermetically closed, then digest it half a year in Horse-dung; then take it out and distill it in *Balneo,* and cohobate the waters till the greatest part of the Brains be distilled off."

Equally potent was The Water of Swallows, a beverage well calculated to reduce the patient's appreciation of good Canary Sack: " Take of Swallows, cut into pieces, the whole birds without seperating anything from them, six ounces, mix the meat togeather well, and add of Castorum cut small an ounce, then infuse them twelve hours in two pints wine, then put them into a glass gourd, and distill them in Sand till all be dry, then Cohobate the Liquor three times." But not even Canary Sack could sweeten this dose: " Take of Cow-dung, fresh, and distill it in *Balneo,* and the water thereof will have the smell of *Ambergriese."* Patent medicines (though unpatented at this early date) were advertised in such pamphlets as THE MOURNER'S CORDIAL AGAINST EXCESSIVE SORROW, a duodecimo volume " very Suitable to be given at Funerals," the author of which was one of Boston's leading clergymen. These medicines excellently cured " the Gripings of Guts, & Wind Cholick " and prevented " that woful Distemper the *Dry Belly Ach,"* all for three shillings the half-pint bottle.

In later years Cotton Mather himself wrote a medical treatise, the *Angel of Bethesda* which, though it remains in manuscript to this day, was in part communicated to the Royal Society and given respectful consideration. It was not startling to men of the seventeenth and early eighteenth century to hear that there was " Rime as well as Reason " in the doctrine, " Stercus et urina medicorum fercula prima " (Dung and urine are the first diet of the doctors). By the rule of homœopathy, yet unborn, like cured like; and the many distempers of the intestines could best be treated by the imbibing of animal excreta, or better yet, human. In this medical book Mather declared human excreta " a Remedy for Humane Bodies that is hardly to be paralleled." And human urine had virtues that exceeded those of all the waters of medicinal springs.

But in his youth, nevertheless, Cotton Mather, who was frequently ill, went with his father to " Lyn " to drink the waters and to pray. In his later years he leaned very heavily on prayer as a cure for sickness; and many an entry in the ponderous diary smacks of still undiscovered Christian Science. He early recorded the remarkable case of " Joan Ellis, a very Godly and deaf Widow about fourscore years of Age " who, borrowing a book of Mather's from her pastor, was led by it to believe that " Christ could, and would, give her, her *Hearing,* and upon this shee had her *Hearing* suddenly restored unto her." More directly did he state his belief that sin was the " Cause of Sickness. And, as I must infer what a *bitter* Thing, all Sin in general is, from the Bitterness which I tast in the Effect of it; so, I must enquire, whether, a *malignant Cold,* bee not the very distemper of my Soul; a *cold* Indisposition to Religion, accompanied by sinful Malignity.

" I must ascribe unto the Lord *Jesus Christ,* the Glory

of my *Deliverance* out of *Sickness*. When Hee *bore my Sins,* on the Cross, then he *bore my Sicknesses*. He has by His obedience, made *Atonement* for the *Sins* for which, God might *make me sick in smiting mee. His Death,* is the Price of my *Health."*

He saved some of his children from death by prayer, holding days of fasting for them; indeed, he believed that some of his children (he had fifteen, of whom only six grew up and only two survived him) died because he did not pray enough for them; they were ill because he was " slothful " in his devotions.

Nevertheless, not unlike modern healers who wear glasses on their eyes and gold crowns on their teeth, he did not always find prayer sufficient. When, in spite of fervid and long-continued devotions, his headaches persisted, he resorted to various compresses and to medicines of which he wrote with bated breath, darkly hinting at their power.

He saw much of sickness all through his life. His father was constantly certain that his death was just around the corner; and so much did his belief impress his oldest son that Cotton Mather bade him eternal farewells on each of his many journeys, and each time welcomed him home with joyful surprise. Mather saw epidemics and accidents carry off his father's friends; he himself along with others of his family was touched with smallpox, that disease from which few were immune. Children were, however, frequently kept to their beds by it only three days. On the tenth day many a child was quite able to come downstairs and join the family at meals and prayers. But there were other childish ills with which Cotton Mather, as the oldest of nine children, only one of whom died in infancy, must have become well acquainted. Babies at this time were prone to " fitts "; and they would manage to suck pins through the silver nipples of their feeding bottles. Disease and accident spared none. The doctor and the minister were needed constantly in all households to add prayer to nauseating medicines.

Mather's interest in medicine never flagged; his knowledge of it helped him through many a crisis in his own household, which staged the birth of fifteen children, the death of two wives and most of the children, and recurrent epidemics of scarlet fever and smallpox. It taught him to study his own physical defects and to attempt to improve them. He listened attentively when he was told that he might overcome his stammer by " a dilated Deliberation in speaking." With the patience of a Demosthenes he persevered until there was no longer room for doubt — he could talk like other men, a little slower, a little more carefully, but time and practice would lessen the stiffness of his tongue and he might yet direct his fellows from the pulpit. Timidly he reopened the subject of his career with his parents.

VI

To the Mathers and their contemporaries the curing of men's souls was an incomparably higher vocation than the curing of their bodies. Cotton Mather as a child had observed the power, social, moral, and political, wielded by his father; he had constantly been told of the importance to the colony of the ministers, his grandparents. He

[49]

had seen his father's power and influence spread. The firſt book published in Boſton had been a sermon of his father's; his father had been urged to accept the presidency of Harvard; his father ever since the boy could remember had been a leader in church and ſtate. Shrewd observer that he was, he recognized the power at the same time that he felt the glory of the miniſtry.

As a matter of faĊt, the ruling caſte of Massachusetts had for nearly fifty years juſtified themselves as the only upholders of a pure and vivid Chriſtianity, fighting with every means at their disposal the conſtant attempts to dilute their clear and concentrated religious power. The chief bulwark of this caſte was the miniſtry, who formed a Supreme Court none the less powerful because it was without express eſtablishment by law. The feeling of respeĊt to the clergy was clearly set forth by John Winthrop, who, in middle age, described the religious experiences of his youth: " Now came I to some peace & comfort in God & in his wayes, my chief delight was therein. I loved a Chriſtian & the very ground he went upon. I honoured a faythful miniſter in my heart & could have kissed his feet: Now I grew full of zeal (which outranne my knowledge & carried mee sometimes beyond my calling), & very liberall to any good work. I had an insatiable thirſt after the word of God & could not misse a good sermon, though many miles off, especially of such as did search deep into the conscience. I had also a great ſtriving in my heart to draw others to God. It pitied my heart to see men so little to regard their soules & to despise that happiness which I knew to be better than all the world besides, which stirred mee up to take any opportunity to draw men to God . . . so that upon the bent of my spirit this way & the success I found of my endeavours, I gave myself up to the study of Divinity, & intended to enter into the ministry, if my friends had not diverted me."

Three years after his graduation Cotton Mather came to another Harvard Commencement, still earnest, still slender of body and tense of mind, still full of the desire to know and the desire to teach, still devoutly subservient to his father, from whose honored hands he now received his M.A., the first touch of the accolade that would eventually raise him to the Knighthood of the Lord.

CHAPTER THREE

"I have no Pleasure comparable to that of doing
Acts of Mercy, Kindness, Goodness. I do them
every Day, and have an Heart insatiably disposed unto the doing of them."

— *The Diary of Cotton Mather*

I

THE Boston into which Cotton Mather had been
born began to change at his very birth. For thirty
years the colony rulers had built up a virtually
independent state, had contrived to keep its direction in
their own hands, had purged the community of any who
had dared to question their power, and had developed a
way of life that in its close conformity to the ideals of its
rulers has never been equaled in this country. And inevi-
tably their death meant the usual cry of those who succeed
in troublous times to men greater than they, regret for
"the giant race before the Flood." From this time dates
the canonization of those New England saints the odor of
whose sanctity reached its fullest efflorescence in the mid-
nineteenth century. The new generation was provincial
with the resourcefulness and ingenuity which provincial
life gives, but also with its narrowness and cocksureness.
Most prominent and least provincial was Cotton Mather's
father, Increase. Cotton Mather was, therefore, in the
midst of a changing life; from his boyhood he could have
watched the thickening storm, which, beginning with the

royal demand for religious freedom for those who wished
to use the book of common prayer, and for the franchise
" to all male freeholders of competent eftate," ended in
1696, when he was twenty-three, in the revocation of the
charter and the transformation of the practically independent ftate of Massachusetts into a dependency of the
crown. More important for the citizenry of Bofton than
the attack upon the charter was the determination of
Charles II to enforce the Navigation Acts designed to
make the colonies commercially valuable to the home
country. There were plenty of Bofton men who were glad
to see public worship with the ceremonial of the eftablished church, but there were none who wished to be told
how and where they were to sell their corn, their codfish,
their lumber, and their rum.

The ftorm finally broke in 1685, when, in spite of faft
days and directions to the minifters " to seek the face of
God for his special guidance and direction," the charter
was condemned in the English courts. In May, 1686, the
new government was eftablished under the presidency of
Joseph Dudley. On May 21ft, wrote Samuel Sewall in his
Diary, " The Magiftrates and Deputies goe to the Governour's. . . . Mr. Nowell prayed that God would pardon each Magiftrate and Deputies Sin. Thanked God for
our hithertos of Mercy 56 years, in which time sad Calamities elsewhere, as Massacre Piedmont; thanked God for
what we might expect from sundry of those now sat over
us. I moved to sing, so sang the 17. and 18. verses of
Habbakuk.

" The Adjournment which had been agreed before

. . . was declared by the Weeping Marshall-Generall. Many Tears Shed in Prayer and at parting." On June 15, 1686, was organized in Boston " the Church of England as by law established "; and on December 19th arrived the first royal governor, Sir Edmund Andros.

II

During the years while the charter was under attack, life in Boston went on much as before. Then, as now, political questions made little difference to the daily routine. The round of agriculture continued; ships loaded their fish, pork, beef, and lumber for the West Indies and brought back sugar, logwood, " silver plate or Amber-groose, or Turtel Shell "; the regulations of the Navigation Acts were variously evaded, and now and then a vessel was captured by pirates, privateers, or " the Algerines."

The populace continued to stray from the right path. Some gentlemen came in a coach from Roxbury to Boston after nine o'clock at night, " singing as they come, being inflamed with Drink: At Justice Morgan's they stop and drink Healths, curse, swear, talk profanely and baudily to the great disturbance of the Town and grief of good people. Such high-handed wickedness has hardly been heard of before in Boston."

Less high-handed were the ordinary run of criminals. " Benjamin Gourd . . . (being about 17 years ot age) was executed for committing Bestiality. . . . The causes he alledged were idleness, not obeying parents, &c." " Sam Guile of Havarel Ravished Goodwife Nash of Amesbury, about G. Bailyes Pasture at the white Bottoms." " A Scotchman and Frenchman kill their Master, knocking him in the head as he was taking Tobako. They are taken by Hew and Cry, and condemned: Hanged." " Stephen Goble . . . was executed for murder of Indians: three Indians for firing Eames his house, and murder. . . . Mr. Mighil prayed; four others sate on the Gallows, two men and two impudent Women, one of which, at least, Laughed on the Gallows, as several testified." " An Indian was branded in Court and had a piece of his Ear cut off for Burglary." " This day about 6 or 7 at night a Male Infant pin'd in a sorry Cloth is laid upon the Bulk of Shaw, the Tobacco-Man: Great Search made tonight and next day to find the Mother."

Children are born, are welcomed joyfully, and die in convulsions; men go chestnuting and dine largely at houses in the country; people fall ill, are generously bled and nauseously dosed; violent winters alternate with open winters; and the ministers preach their vivid sermons and exhort on lecture days.

Certainly life in Boston in 1663 held plenty of material to justify the current belief that life was a bitter struggle between God and the devil for the precious possession of man's soul. Cotton Mather was born into a society which believed that man's soul was worth the struggle that had to be made if it were to be saved from eternal torment. To this struggle his fathers had devoted their lives; for an ultimate victory which it could never doubt an oligarchic state had marshaled all its resources.

III

It is small wonder that Cotton Mather believed himself singularly favored when, by permitting him to overcome his stammer, the Lord admitted him among His chosen servants whose task it was to save men's souls. Adolescence for him, as for many a youth, had led to increased religious fervor, all the insistences of sex sublimated into missionary zeal. He saw the people about him sharply divided into the good, the bad, and the indifferent, all material for the ministerial hand to mold. Even criminals might be saved by repentance; and there were all the indifferents who might be diverted from a life of crime to a life of piety. To influence others is youth's delight; to influence them for good has been an intoxicating thought to many more than the boy Cotton Mather.

He was only seventeen when he preached his first real sermon in his grandfather's Dorchester church. In the still heat of an August day he faced the congregation, most of whom had sat under his grandfather and who remembered him as the great preacher of his time. They listened to the boy in the pulpit with critical attention and they saw in him the promise of true greatness. They saw a slight, nervous youth, his face reflecting the ardent desire to be worthy of his ancestors, worthy of his noble calling, worthy of the divine favor that had raised him to the pulpit. Realizing his youth and inexperience, he had sought long for a suitable text, one which would permit him with his slender experience of life to speak wisdom to men whose weight of years and dignity frightened him.

" He hath sent me to heal the broken-hearted " — here was a text which even a very young man might elucidate for his elders. " He hath sent me to heal the broken-hearted " — here was a chance to refer to his abandoned medical career and make neat references to the art of healing, cross references to body and soul, double meanings dear to the heart of an age that prized anagrams. As the lad talked his nervousness wore off and with it went the stammer that at first impeded his clear utterance. He fell under the intoxication of the platform; the words of his mouth seemed almost inspired. He leaned forward with the direct personal appeal hard for any audience to resist. He felt the congregation rise to the bait he threw them; he was aware of the sympathetic bond between them. To his joy he realized that they were interested; he grew more eloquent watching them respond to his emotional appeal. He saw them nod to one another as if to say, " The true Mather voice." The platform virus coursed in his veins; he was off on an almost incredible career of talking — he saw the years spread before him, years in which he would again and again exhort his fellow men, leading them in the path of holiness. He was not deceived in his vision; in the years to come people liked to listen to him full as well as he liked to talk; and he was to stand at pulpit and on platform innumerable times sermonizing and lecturing more than would seem possible for mortal man.

At seventeen in his grandfather's church he realized with a singing in his heart that upon his slight shoulders would really fall the mantle of the Mathers.

Six months later — though not yet ordained — he became an assistant in his father's church. His training had prepared him for just such a career, dominated by the personality of his father, whose most dutiful son and most ardent advocate he always remained. In 1675, when Cotton Mather was entering Harvard, the first book printed in Boston (hitherto printing was forbidden except in Cambridge) was a sermon of Increase Mather's, showing, doubtless conclusively, " that excesse in wickedness doth bring untimely Death " — such death as Cotton ever feared and for which he tried constantly to be prepared. When he took his B.A. his father was publicly praised; when he took his M.A. he received it from his father's hand. And finally he was ordained by his father. His filial devotion was something extraordinary, beyond the normal demands of the relationship and beyond the normal affection of a son for his distinguished parent. He hardly cared to do more than to magnify or extend his father's ideas. So confident was he always that his father was right that even in his later years he could not encounter anyone with whom Increase was at odds without frothing. The most violent abuse he heaped upon those who spoke disrespectfully of his father; those who reviled himself were lightly abused and speedily forgiven.

As his father's assistant he remained in Boston all his life, traveling only comparatively short distances to preach. With a deep love for his " mother land," he never saw England. His father remained there for some years, his brother settled there, later his own son visited there; he himself remained in Boston in an ever busier round of

[58]

parish duties. He must have longed to go abroad as a young man, if only for adventure; when he was made a Fellow of the Royal Society his desire to go to England to be invested with the honor must have been intense; yet then, as at the beginning of his career, he refused because of his devotion to his father's interests. He could not be spared. His father could travel, could hold public office, because his church was taken care of by this capable and self-sacrificing son. At the very outset of his career Cotton Mather refused a call to New Haven twice, the second time giving as his reason, " because the Church of *North Boston* would have entertained uncomfortable Dissatisfactions at my Father, if after so many importunate *Votes* of theirs, for my Settlement here, hee had any way permitted my Removal from them." And years later this father's health did not *permit* his acceptance of the presidency of Yale College.

At sixteen he had joined the church; at eighteen he was its pastor. At eighteen it must have been thrilling to be an officer of the church; at sixty-five it must have been disappointing to look back over life, having been little else. He had stepped into his father's shoes and they fitted; the Lord never granted him a new pair.

IV

It was not an exciting life for a young man. A typical day noted partly in Latin in his diary ran: " Read Exod. 34, 35, 36, Prayed. Examined the Children. Read Descartes. Read Commentators on Joh. 6.37. Breakfast: Prepared Sermon. Joined Family Prayers. Heard pupils

[59]

Recite. Read Salmon on Medicine: dined. Visited many Friends. Meditation: On *the exceeding Willingness of the Lord Jesus to Do Good unto those that come unto Him;* and, I resolve,

" As to bee encouraged in my Addresses unto the Lord Jesus for His *Mercy,* from the Thoughts of his *Merciful-ness,* thus also to endeavour that I may bee like unto Him in humble and ready *Helpfulness* unto others, Prayed. Supped. Prepared sermon. Joined Family Prayers."

Sermons were among the interesting events of the times, worthy of note in gentlemen's diaries: " Mr. Willard speaks to the 7th Comandment, condemns naked Brests: and seems to be against the Marriage of First-Cousins." " Mr. Mather Preaches . . . that Love was an ingredient to make one zealous: those that received good People received Christ. . . . Said that if the Government of N. E. were zealous might yet save this people." " Isa. 33.17. was preached from. by Mr. Cotton Mather. Thine eyes shall see the King, &c. whoes Sermon was somewhat disgusted for some expressions; as, sweet sented hands of Christ, Lord High Treasurer of Aethiopia, Ribband of Humility — which was sorry for, because of the excellency and seasonableness of the subject, and otherwise well handled." The flowery figures were the imaginings of a youth not much above twenty.

A mere boy, Cotton Mather started his career with the noblest of resolutions. He was determined to be worthy of his ancestry and of the good opinion of his father's parishioners. His eager striving toward worthiness is painful to read. Again and again he recorded his willingness to die, but, if God will, his desire to live and to " *do* something and in thy Time . . . *write* something that may do good unto *young Persons* when I shall bee dead and gone." He could not know that he would leave a bibliography of four hundred and thirty-seven entries, long enough to ſtagger the imagination of young people two centuries after his death. He would not have believed that his fame would laſt far beyond that of the prominent father who towered above him in life. Having no future to seek, with a permanent berth already his, he sought ways to make himself more fit for his position, one which was doubly precious to him because his ſtammer, not yet wholly conquered, had threatened to exclude him from it. He early began his syſtem of secret faſt days, when he uttered long prayers of supplication and thanksgiving. These he planned to hold once a " fourteen night," but even now they sometimes came oftener to the detriment of a naturally frail conſtitution. " How wonderful is the Goodness of God unto mee, a vile Worm, in that Hee does employ mee, in the *Miniſtry* of the Lord Jesus Chriſt."

Early attainment of ambition may make a young man vain or it may make him humble. Cotton Mather was overwhelmed by a sense of gratitude to the God who granted him, for all his unworthiness, so many and so great blessings. He searched his heart, he scrutinized his actions, he regulated his thoughts and days that he might come nearer to his ideal of a Chriſtian. In his diary he noted his methods to do good: " As I walk in the *Street,* or sitt in the *House,* tho' I will not bee so *pharisaical* as to show it, yett I will use frequently to lift up a Cry unto

God, for some *suitable Blessing* to be vouchsafed, unto the Persons I have before mee. . . .

"It has been a frequent Thing to mee, to redeem the *silent,* and otherwise, *thoughtless,* Minutes of my Time, in shaping Thousands of *ejaculatory Prayers* for my Neighbours. . . .

"At a *Table,* where, I being the *youngest* of the Company, it was not proper for *mee* to discourse at all, and the Discourses of *others* were too trivial, to bee worthy of my Attention.

Casting my Eye upon,	Ejaculations.
The Gentlewoman that *carved* for us.	*Lord, carve,* of thy Graces and comforts, a *rich portion,* unto that Person.
A Gentlewoman lately *married.*	*Lord, espouse* and *marry,* the Soul of that Person to thyself, in a Covenant never to be forgotten.
A Gentlewoman very *beautiful.*	*Lord, beautify* the Soul of that Person with *thy Comeliness.*
A Gentlewoman very *gay in her Apparrel.*	*Lord,* give that Person an *humble Mind,* and let her Mind bee most concern'd for the *Ornaments,* that are *of great Price in thy Sight.*

One of our *Magistrates*.	*Lord,* inspire that Person with *Wisdome, Courage,* and *Goodness,* to *seek the Welfare of His People.*

. . . .

One unhappy in his *Children*.	*Lord,* convert the *Children,* of that Person, and lett him have the Joy to see them *walking in thy Truth.*

. . . .

One that hath mett with *great Losses.*	*Lord,* give to that Person, the *good Part,* which *cannot bee taken away.*
A *Servant,* giving Attendance.	*Lord,* make that Person, a *Servant of Jesus Christ.*

" In like Manner, when I have been sitting in a Room full of People, at a *Funeral,* where they take not much Liberty for *Talk,* and where yett much *Time* is most unreasonably lost, I have usually sett my Witts at work, to contrive *agreeable Benedictions,* for each Person in the Company.

" In passing along the *Street,* I have sett myself to *bless* thousands of persons, who never knew that I did it; with *secret wishes,* after this manner sent unto Heaven for them.

[63]

Upon the Sight of	Ejaculations.
A *tall* Man.	*Lord,* give that Man, *High Attainments* in Christianity: lett him fear God, *above many.*
A *lame* Man.	*Lord,* help that Man, to *walk uprightly.*
A *Negro.*	*Lord, wash* that poor Soul *white* in the *Blood* of thy Son.
Children standing together.	*Lord, lett* the *blessing Hands* of my Lord Jesus Chriſt, bee putt upon these *Children.*
Children at *Play.*	*Lord,* lett not these Children always forgett the *Work,* which they came into the World upon.

. . . .

A Man carrying a *Burden.*	*Lord,* help this Man, to carry a *burdened Soul,* unto his Lord-Redeemer.
A Man on *Horseback.*	*Lord,* thy *Creatures* do serve that man; help him to serve his *Maker.*
Young People.	*Lord,* help these Persons to *remember their*

	Creator in the Dayes of their Youth.
Young Gentlewomen.	**Lord,** make 'em *wise Virgins,* as the *polish'd Stones* of thy *Temple.*

.   .   .   .

One whom I *know not:* (and saw no other singular Circumſtance about him, to shape any Thoughts upon.)	**Lord,** lett this Person bee so *known* to, as to bee sav'd by, the Lord.
One who (as I had heard) had spoken very *reproachfully* and *injuriously* of mee.	**Lord,** bless and spare and save that Person, even as *my own Soul.* May *that Person* share with mee, in all the *Salvations* of the Lord.
One that was reckon'd a very *wicked* Man.	**Lord,** rescue that poor Man, from *Satan,* who *leads him captive.*

". . . I have unspeakable Cause, to bless my Lord Jesus Chriſt, for teaching mee, by His Holy Spirit, before I was *twenty years of Age,* these Methods of living unto His glory."

Years later the same desire to find in everything, however mean, a holy purpose, led him to record: " I was once emptying the *Ciſtern of Nature,* and making *Water* at the Wall. At the same Time, there came a *Dog,* who did so too, before me. Thought I: ' What mean, and vile Things are the Children of Men, in this Mortal State! How much do our *natural Necessities* abase us, and place us in some regard, on the same Level with the very *Dogs!* '

" My Thought proceeded. ' Yett I will be a more noble Creature; and at the very Time, when my *natural Necessities* debase me into the Condition of the *Beast,* my *Spirit* shall (I say, *at that very Time!*) rise and soar, and fly up, towards the Employment of the *Angel.*'

" Accordingly I resolved, that it should be my ordinary Practice, whenever I step to answer the one or other *Necessity of Nature,* to make it an Opportunity of shaping in my Mind, some holy, noble, divine *Thought; . . .* a *Thought* that may leave upon my Spirit some further *Tincture of Piety!*

" And I have done according to this Resolution! "

This train of thought persisted until another decade suggested: " There are with me, in common with all the Children of Men, the usual Evacuations of Nature, to be daily attended. I would not only improve the Time which these call for . . . but I would now more particularly study that the Thoughts I form on these Occasions, may be of some *abasing Tendency.* The Actions themselves carry Humiliations in them; and a Christian ought alwayes to think humbly of himself, and be full of self-abasing and self-abhorring Reflections. By loathing of himself continually, and Being very sensible of what are his own loathsome Circumstances, a Christian does what is very pleasing to Heaven. My Life (above any Man's) ought to be filled with such Things: and now I contrive certain Spotts of Time, in which I shall be by Nature itself invited unto them."

These thoughts were not ſtrange in a day when babies a few hours, days, or weeks old were prayed over; when prominent miniſters were summoned to homes where infants lay ill, one praying in the morning, another in the afternoon, and a third in the evening. And when the prayers failed to save a baby's life, its funeral was a sedate affair with due diſtribution of rings and scarves and gloves.

Funerals were diversions, parties to which an invitation was a compliment, the omission of an invitation an affront. Gloves were given largely; rings only to the more important gueſts. There were, then, grades of social favor in the diſtribution of these somber gifts, at a time when diversions were somewhat dependent upon death, disaſter, and crime.

Now and then a Quaker stalked through the town crying, " Repent! Repent! " or with blackened face burſt in upon a Sabbath-day service. In 1685 " a Quaker or two goe to the Governour and ask leave to enclose the Ground the Hanged Quakers are buried in under or near the Gallows, with Poles . . . ," a requeſt denied by the Council because it would be " very inconvenient for persons so dead and buried in the place to have any Monument." Nevertheless, two months later there was noticed on Boſton Common " a few Feet of Ground enclosed with Boards, which is done by the Quakers out of respeℭ to some one or more hanged and buried by the Gallows. . . ." In the good old days the executioner's whip would have drawn Quaker blood for this.

[67]

A dancing master, who held " mixt Dances," had endeavored to set up in Boston during these years, but had been sternly told that this was no time for New England to dance; though one dancing master declared that " by one Play he coulde teach more Divinity than Mr. Willard or the Old Teastament." Cotton Mather's father published *An Arrow against Profane and Promiscuous Dancing out of the Quiver of the Scriptures,* which suffered a re-issue in two years, so threatening was the danger.

Aside from church, lectures, funerals, executions, there were few permissible diversions. There were for gentlemen excursions to the country, little trips by boat, and the mild excitements of bookshops and a " Coffee, tee and Chucaletto " shop, the name of which was later shrewdly changed to " The Sign of the Bible."

At twenty the boy preacher, then, had little to occupy him save to devise means for inceasing his usefulness to his heavenly and his earthly father. He conceived the idea of parish visiting, setting apart one afternoon a week for the purpose. Here and in his organization of religious clubs for young men he showed himself a forerunner of modern ministry.

v

But for all his studiousness and seriousness he was a very human young man with a troublesome body. He prayed the Lord to help him crucify the lusts of his body; he doubled his devotions and his fast days. But his thoughts strayed. In midsummer he noted in his diary: " Using of sacred *Meditations* . . . at my waking Minutes, every Morning, in my *Bed,* and in this Course, going over many Portions of the Scriptures a Verse at a Time, the Thought of *Isaac* having his happy Consort brought unto him, *when* and where, hee was engag'd in his holy *Meditations,* came sometimes into my Mind, and, I had sometimes a ſtrange Perswasion; that there would a Time come, when I should have my *Bed* blessed with such a Consort given unto mee, . . ."

Six months later he was frightened at the persiſtence of such thoughts: " Having newly been acquainted, with a tremendous and an amazing Inſtance, of a Miniſter ſtricken in years, and eminent and remarked all the Countrey over, for a ſtrict Profession of Holiness, who yett has lately fallen into those lascivious Violations of the *Seventh Commandment,* which have given a most infamous Wound unto Religion; my Soul was thereby caſt into exceeding Fears, leſt I, who am a *Young Man,* in my single Eſtate, should bee left by God, unto some Fall, whereby His Blessed Name would suffer. . . . And this the rather, because . . . I am ſtrongly haunted by the *evil Spirit,* with Temptations, that horribly vex my very Soul within mee. For this Cause, I spent this Day, in the mortifying Exercises of a secret Faſt." His troubles continued, however, and he conſtantly felt it necessary to implore the Lord " That I will endeavour to bee always exemplary for my Chaſtitie." At this time his reading in his father's ample library included much that was intereſting scientifically and morally useful, but much also that was disquieting to an adolescent ſtruggling with insiſtent and unsatisfied sex. Even today it is recognized that miniſters muſt have definite and accurate knowledge of the sins by which they are supposedly uncontaminated. Among the books imported by Increase Mather in 1683 were *The Woman's Advocate, or Fifteen real Comforts of Matrimony . . . With Satyrical Reflections on Whoring, and the Debauchery of this Age,* and two copies of *The London Jilt, or the Politick Whore; shewing all the artifices and stratagems which the Ladies of Pleasure make use of, for the intreaguing and decoying of Men; interwoven with several pleasant stories of the Misses' ingenious performances.*

Fortunately, Cotton Mather's thoughts were much occupied by his parish work and his approaching ordination. On Wednesday, May 13, 1685, before a congregation that would be considered vast even today, he " prayed about an Hour and a Quarter, and preached . . . about an Hour and a three quarters." His father ordained him, saying, " my son Cotton Mather, and in's sermon spake of Aaron's Garments being put on Eleazar, intimating he knew not but that God might now call him out of the World." It is small wonder that Cotton Mather ever felt the presence of the angel of death; at all crises in his life his father summoned that angel. Death for Increase was immediately around the corner from the time of his youth; his successful evasion until his eighty-fifth year failed to make him confident.

The young pastor was invited to make one of the ministers who prayed the next week at Samuel Sewall's house during his celebration of a fast. To this fast, beginning " about half an hour past nine," were invited all the magistrates as well as several ministers. Such gatherings were apparently enjoyable. Though one went empty until evening, he must have gained some joy, spiritual and intellectual and doubtless social, from contact with other worthies. And at least no one had to arise early to arrive in time.

The excitement of his ordination, of being invited to preach in the pulpits of his father's friends, of baptizing " the first Child that ever I washed in the Name of the Glorious Trinitie," of administering for the first time " the Lord's-Supper," of " preaching the Country-Lecture " in his " Father's Turn, who keeps at Cambridge " — such lectures were events in Boston — all these activities brought Cotton Mather a temporary respite. Toward the end of the summer, however, he gave up a day to fasting with " *Humiliations* and *Supplications,* especially to seek for the Guidance and Blessing of God, in what concerns the change of my Condition in the World, from single, to married; whereto I have now many Invitations." Handsome, well-dressed young ministers, especially of such superior social standing, have ever found themselves assailed by young ladies who do not sufficiently distinguish between love of God and love of man.

And it was not hard for women to love Cotton Mather. With women he was never oppressed with the self-consciousness that had clouded his associations with men. His intellectual keenness here marked him not for ridicule or envy, but for naïve admiration. Fellow students had resented his magnificent memory, his love of study, and his desire to display his knowledge; young ladies ignorant of Latin and Greek, limited in book knowledge, and looking for husbands, took a different attitude. Moreover, Mather was no haughty, aloof young man. To good looks he united a winsome manner, an eagerness to please, and a willingness to be pleased. His omnivorous reading had stored his unusually retentive mind with a quantity and variety of fascinating facts with which he was always ready to astonish and entertain. He found the world vastly interesting. To his inquiring disposition all things were open for investigation, and whereas in the pulpit he might be limited to matters of spiritual value, in the parlor he was free to delight with quaint and curious lore. When he spoke young ladies blushed and leaned forward to catch his every word. They admired his bearing, his pleasant voice (no trace of stammer now), his sparkling eye, his vivid phrasing. Mather was no ascetic; he enjoyed society; he enjoyed clothes, food, wine, books, conversation. He felt it no sin to use the wit God gave him or to clothe appropriately his God-given body. Before he went abroad each day he stood before the glass to adjust his fashionable raiment and admire his modish periwig. When he heard disparaging comments he preached a sermon in defence of periwigs — somewhat to the scandal of his older and more conservative parishioners. Sackcloth and ashes were, he felt, hardly the normal apparel for man's daily life.

To young ladies he was irresistible. Their fathers praised him, their brothers were obliged to listen to him with respect, their mothers sighed as they placed him at the top of the list of eligible bachelors. As he walked down the streets of Boston he was conscious of the friend-

[72]

liness and respect of the passer-by, and he could not be unaware of the alluring glances from behind window curtains.

His profound reverence for his father kept him from undue vanity — he felt that much of the favor shown him was a tribute to his family rather than to himself. Nevertheless, he could hardly attribute to his ancestors the very obvious favor bestowed upon him by certain attractive young ladies.

Such attentions were disturbing. Another day of prayer speedily became necessary, and now " I professed, that I would study to do nothing hereabout, that should be *Displeasing* unto Him: I declared, that I desired Nothing in this World, which might prejudice my *Glorifying* of Himself: I said, that if Hee saw any thing would *hinder* mee from *honouring* of Him, I should bee glad, if Hee would *hinder* mee from *having* of that, whatever my misguided Appetites, might plead unto the contrary: I said, that if Hee would have mee to embrace a *Coelibacy*, I would evermore take a Contentment in it. . . .

" Nevertheless, to this I subjoined, that since my inclinations and Invitations did now seem to recommend a married Estate unto mee, I begg'd of Him, that *Hee would lead mee in the Way wherein I should go; and I vow'*D unto Him, that if Hee would prevent all Obstructions of my desirable Settlement in a married Relation . . . I will TWICE at least, EVERY YEAR, join . . . in keeping a *Day of Thanksgiving,* privately unto Himself." After all, " *Marriage* was His Ordinance."

And on his twenty-third birthday he made his first call

[73]

on "ABIGAIL, the Happy Daughter of JOHN and KATH-
ARIN PHILIPS." In order to make success certain this
youth recorded that "I propounded unto Myself, the
Methods, . . . wherein the glorious Lord Jesus Chriſt,
engaged our immortal Souls unto Himself; and I ſtudied
how to make my Addresses unto my Friend analogous
unto *those*. But, alas, *wherewithal shall a young Man
cleanse his Way?*"

Poor lad! his deep religious sense and his diſtruſt of the
body bothered him the more as he courted this alluring
fifteen-year-old maiden, flattered by the attentions of the
elegant, learned, and successful young man. "Leſt any
unholiness might gain upon" his heart Cotton held a
weekly faſt day. For him there was no outlet for sexual
tension except prayer. And the gossip juſt now was titil-
lating. A certain captain was tried "for Insufficiency," a
trial cheerily reported by that gay bookseller, Dunton:
"In all such Cases the good Wives are loaded with Im-
pudence, &c. But where's the sence on't? Women are of
the same Species and Composition with our selves, and
have their Natural Inclinations as well as we." At this
time, too, Cotton Mather made one of the punitive council
that dealt with a miniſter convicted of profaneness and
possible adultery. This caused him to reflect, "*What if
God should single mee out now to bee so publickly loaded
with Shame for Sin?*"

Fortunately his wedding day was drawing near. Mind-
ful of an ancient Rabbi who went through his usual
prayers, though "a Bridegroom is free from saying over
his Phylacteries the firſt night," Cotton Mather on his

wedding-morning prayed long; and arriving early in Charlestown, walked in the garden reading and commentating the wedding in the second chapter of John. Two Sundays later he preached on " Divine Delights."

Previous to his marriage he had not failed to pray for a suitable habitation and for an increase of his salary that he might avoid " the Diſtresses and Temptations, which *Poverty* does expose unto." A feeling of delicacy, an unwillingness to compute in money his serviceableness to the Lord, and a combination of pride and humility kept him in his long connection with the church from directly seeking a larger income. He may often have thought, as his father had years before, that his congregation had little heed for his comfort, but, unlike his father, he did not confide this feeling to his diary. He did, however, at times note that he had never asked for anything from the church, even when he was in financial ſtraits. So now at his marriage he referred the matter of his income to the Lord. He had been brought up to believe that all things were the Lord's. There were no insignificant acts in life; whether one chose a vocation or a slave, God's guidance was necessary.

Now at twenty-three Cotton Mather's life was serene. He had won his spurs; he was much sought after as a preacher; his father's congregation took kindly to him; his parish visits were well received; and he was the means of adding several members to the church. He did not relax effort because his way was thus early made for him; he hunted about for more and more work so that by his efforts the influence of the church was spread and the scope of its endeavors widened. Groups of young men met in his study; and Sunday nights he offered to entertain neighbours with prayers and Psalms and résumés of the day's sermons. To his gratification more than a hundred people would come each time. He was now settled in the house into which his father had moved when he was seven years old, and, thanks to his prayers and the more practical men of his congregation, he was freed of financial worries and able to turn his attention to the increasing weight of parish duties which his father left to him.

VI

One occurrence during his courtship must have diverted his thoughts, for on March 6th James Morgan, a condemned murderer, requested that the sermon of his last Sunday on earth be preached by Cotton Mather. For the ungodly at these times there were many amusements — dice, cards, dancing, drinking; for the godly there were the Thursday lectures when great crowds gathered to listen to the minister of the day and to hear the news. Wrong-doers were censured, and sometimes dangerous books were burned. But godly and ungodly joined when condemned criminals were brought to church to be made a warning to all. In church a criminal made his last public appearance before his final one at the gallows. He could get what gratification he could out of his importance. Important he was, for the minister of his choice wrestled with the Lord for his soul, and every person, great and small, seemed to want a look at him. So great were the crowds at times that the largest meeting-house in town could not accommodate them, and masses of people surged in the ſtreets ſtriving for a view.

John Dunton, who loved to draw himself as a chief actor in any human drama, writes to George Larkin, Printer, of London, on March 25, 1686: " Another Occurrence that happened, whilſt I was here, was the Execution of Morgan, which I may send you as a Piece of News, for there has not (it seems) been seen an Execution here this seven years. So that some have come 50 miles to see it: And I do confess, Considering what serious care the two Mathers and Mr. Moody took to prepare the Dying Criminal for Death, the Relation may be worth relateing . . . and in this Occurrence, I shall relate nothing but what I saw myself.

.   .   .   .

Here it was that I saw poor Morgan; who seem'd to be very sorrowful and penitent, and confessed that he had in his rage murdered the Man whose Death and Blood has been laid to his Charge: He told me that the other gave him some ill Language whereby he was provoked, and that he said to him, If he came within the door, he wou'd run the spit into his Bowels, and he was as wicked as his Word. . . .

" But to return to Morgan, whose Execution being appointed on the 11th of March, there was that Care taken for his Soul that three Excellent Sermons were preached before him . . . ; Two on the Lord's Day, and one juſt before his Execution. The firſt was preached by Mr. Cotton Mather, who preached upon that Text in

Isa. 45:22, *Look unto Me and be ye saved, all the Ends of the Earth.* He declar'd that when the no less unexpected than undeniable Request of a Dying Man, who (says he) now stands in this Assembly, that he wou'd allow him this morning, a Discourse proper to his Uncomfortable Circumstances, was brought to him, he cou'd not think of a more proper Text; Telling the poor Wretch, That he was now listening to one of the three last Sermons that ever he was like to sit under before his incounter with the King of Terrors. And then said, ' Poor Man! Do you hearken diligently, and I'll study to make this whole hour very particularly suitable and serviceable to you; and methinks a Man that knows himself about to take an Eternal Farewel of all Sermons, shou'd Endeavour to hear with most Earnest heed.' And a little after, ' The Faithful and True Witness saith unto us, *I will give you rest;* O let the poor fetter'd Prisoner recollect himself! James! Thy name is not excepted in these Invitations.

" ' I am glad for the seemingly penitent Confession of your montstrous Miscarriages, which yesterday I obtained in writing from you, and which indeed was no more than there was need of: But it remains yet, that you give your Dying Looks to the Lord Jesus Christ; for Salvation from all your Guilt. . . .' And a little after, ' My request to you is, That you wou'd at this hour think of an Interest in Christ. — Surely when the Executioner is laying the Cold Cloth of Death over your Eyes, the Look, with the Shriek of your Soul, will then say, " O now a Thousand Worlds for an Interest in Jesus

[78]

Christ!" Surely a few minutes after that, when your naked Soul shall appear before the Judgment-Seat of the Most High, you will again say, an Interest in Jesus Christ, is worth whole Mountains of Massive Gold!

"'You have murder'd the Body and (no thanks to you, if not) the Soul of your Neighbour too: And O that the Rock in your Bosom might flow with Tears at such a thought! If the Court shou'd say unto you, Beg hard, and you shall live; O, how affectionate wou'd you be! Poor dying man, the Lord Jesus Christ saith the same thing to you, If thou canst heartily look and beg, thou shalt not be hang'd up among the Monuments of my Vengeance, in Chains for Evermore.

"'The sharp Ax of Civil Justice will speedily cut you down; O for a little good Fruit before the Blow! Manifest your penitence for your Iniquities by a due care to excel in Tempers quite contrary to those ill habits and Customs whereby you have heretofore blasphemed the Worthy Name of Christ and Christianity: Especially employ the last minutes of your Life, in giving a Zealous Warning unto others, to take heed of those things which have been destructive unto you. Tell them what wild Gourds of Death they are, by which you have got your bane; point out before them those Paths of the Destroyer which have led you down So near unto the Congregation of the Dead.

"'When the numerous Crowd of Spectators are, three or four days hence, throng'd about the Place where you shall then breathe your last before them all, then do you with the heart-piercing-groans of a deadly wounded

[79]

Man, beseech of your Fellow sinners, That they wou'd turn now every one from the Evil of his way. Beseech them to keep clear of ill haunts and ill houses, with as much dread of them, as they cou'd have of lying down in a Neſt of poysonous Snakes: Beseech them to abhor all Uncleanness, as they wou'd the Deep Ditch which the abhorred of the Lord do fall into. Beseech of them to avoid all Excess in Drinking, as they wou'd not rot themselves with more bitter Liquors than the Waters of Jealòusie. Beseeech them to mortifie and moderate all inordinate Passions, as they wou'd not surrender themselves into the hands of Devils, that will hurry them down into deeper Deeps than they are aware of. Beseech them to shun Idle Swearing, as a Prophanity that the God to whom vengeance belongeth will not permit to go unpunished. Beseech them to avoid Curses on themselves or others, leaſt whilſt they like Madmen so throw about Fire-Brands, Arrows, and Death, they bring upon their own heads, as you have done, the things which they are apt to be wishing. Beseech them to beware of Lying, as they wou'd not be put to need, and Crave, and be deny'd, a drop of Water, to cool their Tongues in the place of Torment. Beseech of them to be as averse to all stealing, as they wou'd be to carry coals of Fire into those Neſts that they so feather by their dishoneſty. Beseeech of them to prize the means of Grace; to sleep at, or keep from sermons no more: To love the Habitation of GOD's House, and the place where his Honour dwells; leſt GOD soon send their barren froward souls to dwell in silence, where there shall never be a Gospel-Sermon heard;

[80]

Never, Never, as long as the Almighty sits upon his Chriſtal Throne.

"'And when you have given these Warnings, upon the Ladder from whence you shall not come off without taking an Irrecoverable ſtep into Eternity; O remember ſtill, you give onto Jesus Chriſt the Honour of Looking to him for his salvation. Remember, that if you wou'd do a work highly for the Honour of Him, this is The Work of GOD, that you believe on Him. Even after your Eyes are so covered, as to take their leave of all sights below, ſtill continue Looking unto Him whom you heard saying, *Look unto me*. And now let the Everlaſting Saviour look down in much mercy upon you: O that he wou'd give this Murderer and Extraordinary Sinner, a place among the Wonders of Free Grace! O that this Wretched Man might be made meet for the Inheritance among the Saints in Light; being kept from an unrepenting and deluded Heart, as unquenchable Fire will find fewel in.'

" This was the Subſtance of what Mr. Cotton Mather address'd to the Prisoner, in his Sermon in the Morning."

And as Dunton undoubtedly quoted directly from the published sermons of the two Mathers and Mr. Moodey, his account is for once reliable, even though he may have intermixed the content of all three.

VII

But political affairs also claimed the young miniſter. Stirring indeed were the years from 1686 to 1692 when Governor Andros ruled the Dominion of New England, when Boston had its first revolution, and when Increase Mather negotiated a new charter for Massachusetts.

When the frigate *Kingfisher* in the bleak December weather of 1686 brought Sir Edmund Andros as governor of the Dominion of New England, Boston men were ready to look upon him as a tyrant, emissary of a king who had stolen from them power over a colony which owed nothing to him or to his forbears. Cotton Mather was then twenty-three. Increase, his father, at forty-seven, was in the prime of life. Both became the implacable enemies of the new governor. His " Scarlet Coat, laced," the sixty " Red-Coats " of his guard, the royal frigates in Boston harbor, the firing of great guns on a sacrament Sunday to celebrate the beginning of the third year of the reign of King James, the governor's insistence upon holding Episcopal services in the South Church, the prosecution of Ipswich recalcitrants who had refused to levy taxes, all these, and the many changes due to a new scheme of centralized government, were enough to gain a stern, efficient military man a reputation for tyranny.

A little more than a year after his arrival, the governor's wife died. Her state funeral made a great impression. One worthy Bostonian wrote: " Between 4. and 5. I went to the Funeral of the Lady Andros having been invited by the Clark of the South-Company. Between 7. and 8. . . . The Corps was carried into the Herse drawn by six Horses. The Souldiers making a Guard from the Governour's House down the Prison Lane to the South-M. House, there taken out and carried in at the western dore, and set in the Alley before the pulpit with six Mourning women by it. House made light with candles and Torches; was a great noise and clamor to keep people out of the House, that might not rush in too soon. I went home, where about nine a clock I heard the Bell toll again for the Funeral. It seems Mr. Ratcliff's Text was, Cry, all flesh is Grass.''

While Andros was busily consolidating the Dominion government, his enemies were laying their plans. In April, 1688, Increase Mather left for England as representative of the colony, leaving his church in charge of his son. The twenty-five-year-old minister was equal to the task of leadership that his father's absence entailed, for a year later, when news came of the landing of the Prince of Orange in England, it was at Cotton Mather's house that a New England revolution was arranged. The plan seemed to be for the leading men of Boston to await a popular uprising against Andros. Then, at the proper moment, in the interests of law and order, the members of the oligarchy which had been deposed by the Andros government would come forward and read a declaration composed in advance, presumably by Cotton Mather, reciting the wrongs suffered by New England men and the tyranny of the royal governor. The revolution proceeded according to schedule, with Cotton Mather an excited participant. What the state of his mind was on this dangerous occasion — for this uprising against royal authority would be high treason punishable by hanging, drawing, and quartering if William should be unsuccessful in England — may be inferred from his own account which still throbs with the excitement of those thrilling days:

" By the eighteenth of April, 1689, things were pushed on so far by the people, that certain persons first seized the captain of the frigot, and the rumor thereof running like lightning through Boston, the whole town was immediately in arms, with the most *unanimous resolution* perhaps that ever was known to have inspired any people. They then seized those wretched men, who by their innumerable *extortions* and *abuses* had made themselves the objects of universal hatred; not giving over till the governour himself was become their prisoner; the whole action being managed without the least bloodshed or plunder, and with as much *order* as ever attended any *tumult,* it may be, in the world. Thus did the New-Englanders assert their title to the common rights of Englishmen; and except the plantations are willing to degenerate from the temper of true Englishmen, or except the revolution of the whole English nation be condemned, their *action* must so far be justified." Here is the ring of Boston patriotism which in less than a century was once more to organize and justify a revolution.

With Andros and his officers in confinement Boston quieted down. That the Boston mob showed its usual spirit of merrymaking in the moment of their triumph may be seen in the complaints of the Andros sympathizers in England. The little chapel of the Established Church was apparently a target, for an English pamphlet complains: " the church itself had great difficulty to withstand their fury, receiving the marks of their indignation and scorn by having the Windows broke to pieces and the Doors and Walls daubed and defiled with dung and other filth in the rudest and basest manner imaginable, and the Minister for his safety was forced to leave the country and his congregation and go for England."

The members of the old charter government resumed their power and with Increase Mather to plead their case at the court of the new king, they hoped for the best. But in 1690 Andros and his officers were returned to England, where their side of the case was shown; and it soon became clear that a return to the old independence of the colony was impossible. The diplomacy of Increase Mather and of the two other agents who had become associated with him was taxed to the utmost to secure as favorable terms as possible.

Meanwhile Boston was having its troubles. As Cotton Mather wrote: " New-England was miserably *briared* in the perplexities of an Indian war; and the savages in the *east* part of the country, issuing out from their inaccessible swamps, had for many months made their cruel depredations upon the poor English planters, and surprized many of the plantations on the frontiers into ruin." Their depredations were laid to the influence of the French. Accordingly, it was proposed to damage French influence by making an attack upon Acadia. Under Sir William Phips, the romantic sailor and treasure-hunter, one of the earliest New Englanders to exemplify the American idea that a poor farmer boy has a better chance to rise to power than a rich man's son, the attack was carried out expeditiously and with entire success. To the romance of Phips was now added public confidence in his military prowess, the more so since only a month before the expedition, he had " in the congregation of North-Boston given himself up, ' first unto the Lord, and then unto his people '" and had been baptised by Cotton Mather.

Since the victory over Acadia had been easy, it was determined to send an expedition by land to capture Montreal and an expedition by sea to capture Quebec. Neither came to anything, and in three months Phips was back in Boston with some of his ships lost, with many of his men dead, and more sick. It was a sad day for Boston when the wretched shattered expedition returned. Worst of all, the government was practically bankrupt and the soldiers ready to mutiny. Paper money was issued, but the soldiers "were great sufferers, and could get no more than twelve or fourteen shillings in the pound." As usual, the men with capital made money, for, " As the time of payment of the tax approached, the credit of the notes was raised; and the government allowing five per cent to those who paid their taxes in notes, they became better than money. This was gain to the possessor, but it did not restore to the poor soldier what he had lost by the discount." Back to farms and shops went the soldiers, sick of war, and off to England sailed Sir William Phips to work up interest in a bigger and better expedition against Canada.

Meanwhile Increase Mather's diplomacy was winning for Massachusetts a new charter, and by 1691 a settled government was assured, with a royal governor, a popu-

[86]

lar assembly, and a franchise based not upon religious faith, but upon property qualifications. Sir William Phips was appointed governor and Increase Mather's victory was complete. Phips and Mather, returning to Boston in 1692, were received with ceremony; and with Increase at the summit of his power and influence, Cotton once more dwelt in the shadow of his father.

For Cotton Mather his father's return, in spite of his own immediate loss of importance, was one of the greatest events of his life. During these troublous years he had been the clerical leader of the Boston colonial party; he had planned, preached, and written in their interest; and at the same time he had attended faithfully to the minute affairs of a populous parish. In his rejoicing over his father's return and his successful mission there is no trace of regret for his own passing power: " I am now to receive the Answers of so many *Prayers* as had been employ'd for my absent Parent; and for the Deliverance and Settlement of my poor Countrey, for which hee had been employ'd, in so long an Agencie.

" We have not our former *Charter,* but wee have a *better* in the Room of it. One which much better suits our Circumstances. And instead, of my being made a Sacrifice to wicked *Rulers,* all the *Councellours* of the Province, are of my own Father's Nomination; and my *Father-in-Law,* with several *related* unto mee, and several *Brethren* of my own church, are among them. The *Governour* of the Province is not my *Enemy,* but one whom I baptised, namely *Sir William Phips,* . . . one of my dearest Friends. . . .

[87]

" Oh! what shall I render to the Lord, for all His Benefits! "

And with complete selflessness he stepped back into a subordinate position. In his filial loyalty he had never thought to seize the power and the glory for himself. His had been the pious task of holding the ship for his father.

In 1690 he had been made a member of the Corporation of Harvard, a signal honor for so young a man. But in these days of important affairs he did not let the significance of little things escape him. When he heard a clock strike, he endeavored to find sentiments of striking religious purport; when he put on his winter garments he not only felt grateful to God for so providing for his comfort, but felt it necessary to clothe his soul with warmer spiritual thoughts.

The birth of three daughters and the death of the first-born led to serious reflections. Here was Cotton Mather's first opportunity of making his own sorrow an occasion for benefit to others. In the course of a life during which he lost two wives and thirteen children he preached many a funeral sermon in which personal pain lent dignity and weight to faith.

But already Cotton Mather had become involved in the events which led up to a startling crime wave when the devil in the person of a little black man walked abroad, when a Witches' Sabbath was held in a minister's pasture, when Boston jails were crowded with suspected men and women and even children, and when Salem Village stepped into the limelight with a series of spectacular trials and wholesale hangings.

CHAPTER FOUR

"But my Prayers did especially insist upon the horrible *Enchantments*, and *Possessions*, broke forth
upon *Salem Village:* things of a most prodigious
Aspect. A good Issue to those Things, and my
own Direction and Protection thereabout, I did
especially petition for."

Diary of Cotton Mather

I

SINCE public memory demands a scapegoat for each
blameworthy occurrence, Cotton Mather's name
has always been associated to his discredit with the
Salem Witchcraft. Actually he took no such leading part
in the tragedy as that taken by his fellow ministers, fiery-
tongued orators who felt, as he did, that their service in
the army of the Lord demanded at this time especially
active warfare against the devil. America had been the
territory of the devil until the servants of God had come
to drive him out. Witches were in covenant with the
devil; witchcraft had a recognized history stretching back
to the dawn of time. Against it all ministers had to be
on their guard.

Human interest in evil has never flagged since Eve
gave ear to the devil's advice. From then until today,
when Satan is a star in the movies, he has stood for romance
in the hearts of the multitude. To those who themselves
would never give him audience, his machinations have
been of particular interest; and in the performances and

sufferings of his worshipers and victims, the virtuous have always taken vicarious satisfaction.

Hence to the Puritans the devil was of the utmost importance. In his exploits they enjoyed the imaginary sowing of wild oats. Men of Massachusetts had to take their pleasures where they could. When their babies died theye could look into the tombs and be " entertain'd " with a view of their relatives and admire the disposition of the coffins, feeling, " 'Twas an awful yet pleasing Treat." The pleasures of funerals paled before the pursuit of criminals. More exciting than child-murder, adultery, or heresy was the crime of witchcraft. Here were people who trafficked evilly not with men or beasts, but with the very devil. In this one crime curiosity could never be wholly satisfied; something here passed human knowledge — unless one also became a servant of Satan.

For the devil was a very real person. He had been seen and conversed with. A girl who had as a child been captive to the Indians came in contact with him; and obligingly described him to Cotton Mather, drawing upon an imagination helped along by her knowledge of Indians. Presumably she had had access to no books about the devil; hence her description's coincidence with accepted beliefs was highly valuable. ". . . the Divel that visited her was just of the same Stature, Feature, and complexion with what the Histories of the Witchcrafts beyond-sea ascribe unto him; he was a wretch no taller than an ordinary Walking-Staff; hee was not of a Negro, but of a Tawney, or an Indian colour; hee wore an high-crowned Hat, with strait Hair; and had one Cloven-

FRONTISPIECE OF PART II OF GLANVILL's *Saducismus Triumphatus*, LONDON, 1681

Foot." The number of people who had seen him, and who agreed with this description, was large. To deny him was to deny God. And since he must have agents to work his will upon earth, it were folly to deny witches. " No witches, no immortality, no God! " wrote a passionate defender of witchcraft. Witches existed — they were in the Bible.

The Bible said, " Thou shalt not suffer a witch to live." So in 1641 when John Cotton drew up for the Bay Colony *The Body of Liberties,* a group of laws each based upon Scripture with the Biblical reference carefully noted, he included this against witches labeled, " Deut. xiii, 6, 10 — xvii, 2, 6, Ex. xxii, 20." Although their charter called for laws based upon English law, the colonists preferred to lean on the laws of Moses. There is no evidence to show that the crime of witchcraft had already been detected; and whereas Plymouth Colony first had such a law, no one in Plymouth was ever executed as a witch.

If witches were criminals, it was necessary to know " who was witch." A witch had been defined by an early writer as " a hagged old Woman, living in a little rotten Cottage, under a Hill, by a Wood-side, and must be frequently Spinning at the Door: she must have a black Cat, two or three Broom-Sticks, an Imp or two, and two or three diabolical Teats to suckle her Imp." Just as in a man-hunt anyone who runs away is a criminal, anyone who isn't pure white is a " nigger," so in a witch-hunt anyone some one didn't like was a witch. The rotten Cottage, the Hill and Wood-side, even the cat and the

[91]

spinning, could be dispensed with. But the diabolical teats were subject for investigation no less morbid because in the interests of science and virtue. These were excrescenses that when pricked neither caused pain nor drew blood; they were usually on the privy parts. From them the witch's imp or imps sucked nourishment during the night. Presumably an imp could not go without nourishment for more than twenty-four hours. Hence a pleasant and practically sure way of detecting a witch was to tie her, duly exposed, to a chair or table and so keep her for twenty-four or forty-eight hours. In that time her imp would have to come. For his ingress and egress a hole would be cut in the door, and the curious and righteous could watch hidden. As the imp came only in the dark, the watcher's eyes and imagination had to be equally keen. Cotton Mather himself, though " farr from vrging the vn-English method of torture " to obtain confessions, advised the searching for these teats. " I adde, why should not Witch-markes be searched for? The propertyes, the qualityes of those markes are described by divers weighty writers. I never saw any of those marks, but it is doubtlesse not impossible for a chirurgion, when he sees them, to say what are magicall, & if these become once apparent, it is apparent that these witches haue gone so farre in their wickedness as to admit the most cursed Succages, whereby the Divels haue not onely fetched out of them, it may be the Spiritts of which they make vehicles, wherein they visitt the afflicted, but also they haue infused a venome into them which Exalts the malignity of their spiritts as well as of their bodyes: & it is likely, that by

[92]

meanes of this ferment they would be found Buoyant (if the water-Ordeal were made vpon them)."

The water-ordeal was, however, less popular than it had once been, when Matthew Hopkins, England's infamous witch-finder, in 1644–45 traveled about England collecting some two hundred rewards of twenty shillings (his price per witch) before he was finally executed himself, fourteen months later. From 1648 to 1653 there were thirty witches executed in England; during the Protectorate only six; with the Restoration there was a revival of persecution. In the 'seventies there were for the most part acquittals; in the 'eighties the trials for witchcraft showed a marked decline.

Many were the books written on the subject. At various times Increase and Cotton Mather cite nearly thirty books on witchcraft, not all of which were in defense of its existence. Cotton Mather owned " a book which pretends to prove ' that there are no witches.' " Perhaps this was the book of that sane and enlightened Reginald Scot who in the sixteenth century tried to explain the cry of " Witch! " Friendless old women, he said, were wont to curse at them that refused them aid; to their curses were laid any subsequent illnesses or misfortunes, especially as the physicians, when baffled by a disease, frequently ascribed it to witchcraft. Physicians were not necessarily men of education or even wide knowledge in their field. In a much later day, almost at the end of the first quarter of the eighteenth century, Boston boasted only one doctor holding a medical degree; and that one opposed Cotton Mather in the latter's fight for

inoculation against small pox. In 1584 Scot wrote:
" Witchcraft and Inchantment is the Cloke of Ignorance." A woman sometimes " confesseth that shee (as
a Goddes) hath brought such things to passe, Wherein,
not onlie she, but the Accuser, and also the Justice, are
fowlie decieved and abused . . . that she hath doone or
can doo that which is proper onelie to God himself."
This disposed of the boasters of whom there seems always
to have been a ready supply in both Englands. As for
minor matters, such as the bewitchment of the cream
so that the " Butter will not come," that is especially
true " if either the Maids have eaten up the Cream; or
the Good-wife have sold the Butter before in the Market."
Scot had no belief in either witches or the guilelessness
of human beings.

King James, however, was of a different mind. His
Daemonologie, published in 1593, some time before his
accession to the throne, followed the most bigoted ideas of
the time. His Majesty's delight in hearing confessions
and details of wickedness helped along the persecutions.
But in America by far the more influential writers upholding the honor and necessity of witch-baiting were
Bernard, Perkins, and Glanvil. Joseph Glanvil's book is
especially interesting because of its method. He takes all
the objections to witchcraft and answers them one by one.
Scot's *Discoverie of Witchcraft* he dismisses as " a Far-
rago " too ridiculous to answer; its *" Reasonings* are
trifling and *Childish."* To such arguments as that the
devil ought to be able to save his agents from temporal
justice and that the devil must be too busy with other

mischief to have time to satisfy the luſts of old women, he replies that " the *Devil* who is *wicked* " is " also *unwise.*" If there are no witches then " the *graveſt* and *wiseſt Judges* have been *Murderers,* and the *sageſt* persons *Fools,* or *designing Impoſtors.*" Those who could believe this are " more *credulous* than those whose *credulity* they reprehend," unless they have proof — which obviously they neither have nor can have — that there are no witches. On the other hand, continues Glanvil, " We have the *atteſtation* of thousands of eye and earwitnesses " among them the wise and grave and not only the " easily-deceivable vulgar."

II

In New England the hiſtory of witchcraft before 1692 is simple. Some colonies swung entirely free of the superſtition. The New Haven colony permitted two executions, the laſt in 1653. Various places in Connecticut and Massachusetts had occasional accusations and trials; Hartford and Boſton each executed a woman in 1648. Between the firſt execution in 1648 and 1691, when Mary Randall of Springfield was accused and bound over with her father's guaranty for her good behavior, there were ten executions out of approximately thirty-eight cases. The others resulted in acquittals or were allowed to lapse, with a few inſtances of whipping and transportation.

The firſt execution in Boſton was that of Margaret Jones, who acted as physician, curing her patients by such simple medicines that their effect muſt have depended upon magic. The case of Mrs. Hibbins, a magistrate's widow, caused great dissatisfaction which continued after her execution, the second in New England. Mrs. Hibbins was a woman of intelligence and wealth, whose husband, a prominent man in the colony, died with something less of an estate than she had expected. She had some disputes over the settlement of her property. And " the natural crabbedness " of her temper " made her turbulent and quarrelsome, brought her under church censures, and at length rendered her so odious to her neighbours as to cause some of them to accuse her of witchcraft. The jury brought her in guilty, but the magistrates refused to accept the verdict; so the cause came to the general court, where the popular clamour prevailed against her, and the miserable old woman was condemned and executed. Search was made upon her body for tetts, and in her chests and boxes for puppets, images, &c. but there is no record of any thing of that sort being found." So whereas witches supposedly had teats, whereas they supposedly made puppets to represent their victims, an injury to the puppet causing a like injury to the person represented, the lack of either or both of these characteristics saved no one.

In 1684 a less delicately bred woman in Hadley came to grief, when " Philip Smith, a judge of the court, a military officer, and a representative of the town of Hadley, . . . (an hypocondriac person) fancied himself under an evil hand, and suspected a woman, one of his neighbours, and languished and pined away, and was generally supposed to be bewitched to death. While he lay ill, a number of brisk lads tried an experiment upon the old woman. Having dragged her out of the house, they hung her up until she was dead, let her down, rolled her some time in the snow, and at laſt buried her in it, and there left her, but it happened that she survived, and the melancholy man died."

In 1652 John Bradſtreet was tried at Ipswich " upon his presentment of the laſt court for suspition of haueing familiarity with the devill upon examgnation of the case they found he had tould a lye which was a seconde being convicted once before. The court sets a fine of 20 shillings or else to be whipt." At Salem in 1674 " Chriſtopher Browne haueing reported that he had been trafing or discoursing with one whome he apprehending to be the Deuill. which came like a Gen^t in order to his binding himselfe to be a servant to him, upon his examination his discourse seeming inconsiſtent with truth &c.: the court giuing him good councell & caution for the present dismiss him."

In Pennsylvania there are but two cases on record. In 1684 Governor Penn himself charged the jury who " went forth, and upon their Returne Brought her in Guilty of haueing the Comon fame of a witch, but not guilty in manner and forme as Shee ſtands Indicted." Governor Penn is supposed to have said that there was no ſtatute againſt being *thought* a witch or againſt riding on a broomſtick.

In all the cases previous to 1692 the accused, though not always " hagged old women," were objects of suspicion. Those who were not poor, whether beggars or town scolds, were either boaſtful men, or women of biting tongue who fell afoul of their neighbours. Moreover, the accusations were sporadic.

The Salem persecutions were continual, and though they started with forlorn, poverty-stricken women, they soon passed to pious, God-fearing church members, including one minister of the gospel. Men and women of substance and high standing were accused. The son and namesake of John Alden was arrested. "There stands Alden," shouted those who charged him with witchcraft, "a bold fellow, with his hat on, sells powder and shot to the Indians, lies with the sqaws, and has papooses." Finally the wife of Governor Phips was accused, that gentle lady who in her husband's absence herself signed an order releasing a prisoner suspected of witchcraft. And the wife of the Reverend Mr. Hale, himself a most ardent persecutor, was cried out upon.

No witch or wizard was, however, burned in America. One man, for refusing to plead at court, was pressed to death; the other nineteen victims of the Salem hysteria were, like all other executed witches in this country, hanged.

Though there was plenty of written evidence of the presence and powers of witches, though it was believed that the Indians were the people of the devil, that this country had definitely been the devil's province previous to the coming of godly white men, there was no wave of persecution to which to attribute the Salem outbreak. Here at Salem Village, a small settlement now the town of Danvers, the numbers of those accused in the summer of 1692 went well past the hundred mark — estimates vary from one hundred and fifty to three hundred — sufficient to crowd the jails of Salem and Boston. Up to this time there had been in America occasional accusations followed sometimes by executions, but mostly by acquittals; and there had been men and women who boasted of their commerce with the devil. Increase Mather had devoted part of his book on *Illustrious Providences* (published in 1684) to cases of witchcraft, since witchcraft was a subject for the attention of divines and of scientists. His son Cotton was filled with a scientific zeal that attempted to understand all phenomena, natural, supernatural, and diabolical. Hence when in 1688 John Goodwin of Boston called in the ministers of the town to help him conquer the afflictions of his children, due to their having been bewitched, Cotton Mather made a thorough investigation of this " very stupendous witchcraft." An account of it published at the time and later incorporated in Mather's *Magnalia* is headed *Haec ipse miserrima vidi* (these most wretched things I myself have seen). This publication written, it must be remembered, by a leading minister of Boston, giving importance to the pranks of children who may have been epileptic but who certainly were naughty, must shoulder a great part of the blame for the Salem occurrences.

Cotton Mather at this time was a young man whose first child had been born the year before; he seemed not to remember from his own youth or that of his brothers and sisters the possibilities of naughtiness in children. Like his fellow ministers, he regarded the actions of the four Goodwin children as impelled by some mysterious

[99]

force. The Goodwins, in modern manner, sent their washing out. Because their washerwoman lost, mislaid, or stole a few pieces of linen Goody Glover, a poor Irishwoman, a Roman Catholic in a land of intolerance, was hanged. This " scandalous Irish woman," the mother of the laundress, expressed herself vigorously when the thirteen-year-old Goodwin girl made the accusation of theft. After her " bad language " " the child was immediately taken with odd fits, that carried in them something *diabolical*. It was not long before one of her sisters, with two of her brothers, were horribly taken with the like fits, which the most *experienc'd* physicians pronounced extraordinary and preternatural." The youngest child was relieved after the ministers of Boston and Charlestown had held a " day of prayer with fasting . . . at the troubled house," but as the other children continued in their torments, Goody Glover was hanged.

These children were sometimes " *deaf,* sometimes *dumb,* sometimes *blind,* and often all this at once." Their jaws and limbs were thrown out of joint; their necks were sometimes seemingly broken, sometimes stiffened extraordinarily. They were " cut with *knives,* and struck with *blows."* Moreover, these children wouldn't go to bed when they were sent. They wouldn't sit still during sermons and prayers. They were rude to their elders. They barked like dogs and acted like puppies. They purred like cats and scratched like kittens. They flew like geese — one flew across a room " about 20 foot, . . . (as 'tis affirmed) none seeing her feet all the way touch the floor." They would pretend to jump over high fences.

" It would sometimes cost one of them an Hour or Two to be undrest in the evening or drest in the morning. For if any one went to unty a string, or undo a Button about them, or the contrary; they would be twisted into such postures as made the thing impossible . . . nor could they go to wash their Hands, without having them clasp't so odly together, there was no doing of it. But when their Friends were near tired with Waiting, anon they might do what they would unto them. . . . If one ordered them to Rub a clean table, they were able to do it without any disturbance; if to rub a dirty Table, presently they would with many Torments be made uncapable. And sometimes, tho but seldome, they were kept from eating their meals. . . . But nothing in the World would so discompose them as a Religious Exercise." However, " about Nine or Ten at Night they alwaies had a release from their miseries, and . . . slept all night."

Cotton Mather investigated the case thoroughly; he prayed for and with these children; he took into his own home the oldest girl, sufficiently wily to play her part even more violently to justify this attention. She walked with the weight of the chains that were fastened to Goody Glover's leg; she would be choked by an invisible rope; she would have to be deterred from jumping down the well to rescue some silver she declared to be at its bottom. Cotton Mather, having recently bought the house, knew of no such silver; but the former owner of it came in opportunely to declare that some had been lost down the well many years before. The girl, moreover, declared " That if she might but steal or be drunk, she should be well immediately." She would knock at Mather's " study door, affirming ' that some below would be glad to see me,' though there was none that ask'd for me. And when I chid her for telling what was false, her answer was, ' Mrs. Mather is always glad to see you! ' " This " sawciness " of hers coupled with her habit of throwing things at him and her " hectering " of him, made the young minister feel that she must be inspired by the devil. He had been accustomed to respect from young and old since he was in his teens; no sane person would so affront him. She would attempt to " fetch blows with her fist, and kicks with her foot," at him when he prayed, though fortunately these blows and kicks " would always recoyl, when they came within an inch or two of him, as if rebounding against a wall." Her voice, however, was not thus stopped and she " would whistle, and sing, and yell, to drown the voice of prayer." Sacred books and " especially . . . catechisms " she could not read; " books of jests," however, she could read " well enough, and have cunning descants upon them." Popish books and Quaker books (Mather was no friend to the Quakers!) caused her no trouble; but books against Quakers or against Popery the daemons would not permit her to read. She could not read a " book which proves ' that there are witches,' " but could read one " which pretends to prove ' that there are no witches.' "

On Christmas day this girl at the Mather house and her sister at home were made " very drunk " " by the daemons," though they had no " *strong drink* to make them so." The girl's explanation was that the daemons

[102]

were making her keep Christmas with them — at this time the keeping of Christmas was regarded as irreligious, pagan, illegal; the law requiring shops to be open and forbidding heathenish celebration. Saying that the daemons, being unable to do anything worse, were determined to disgrace her, this girl gave way to her drunkenness. " And immediately the ridiculous behaviours of one drunk were, with a wondrous exactness, represented in her *speaking,* and *reeling,* and *spewing,* and anon *sleeping,* till she was well again." Although later bewitched girls managed to swallow rum when the daemons prevented their taking food for days together, it seemed never to occur to the Puritans, who always drank freely themselves, that they had perhaps a liquor problem to deal with. The Goodwin girls seemed for a time to have drunk the devils out of them; but when their afflictions returned Cotton Mather " perfected " their deliverance by three days of prayer.

The prominence given the pranks of these children by all the ministers, and the special attention of this eminent though youthful minister, must have been the well-spring of the Salem witchcraft. Just as the Goodwin children aped the pranks performed by English children when Matthew Hale tried the witches of Suffolk, so the Salem girls based their performances on those of their predecessors. Such similarity of action of all these children to one another and to the recorded cases of Hale did not awake suspicion; to Boston men it was rather a convincing proof that the devil acted the same now and forever.

III

Such hysterical outbreaks as that at Salem Village require small foundation; they can build upon the shifting sands of popular interest. The case of the Goodwin children was sufficiently strong to hang poor Goody Glover, their bewildered victim, whose Catholic answering to Protestant questioning seemed a complete confession. Cotton Mather in his report stated that several *"poppets,* or babies, made of raggs, and stuffed with goats' hair " were found in her house; " and the vile woman confessed that her way to torment the objects of her malice, was by wetting of her finger with her spittle, and stroaking of those little images." Nevertheless, Mather prayed for her and questioned her further about her diabolical practices until her execution, when at the last she said " the afflicted children should not be reliev'd by her death."

But the victim was not the object of interest that the afflicted children were. Their exploits were read and talked of in many places. And it was perfectly natural that children, with their normal love of dramatic action and their normal love of attracting attention, should proceed to imitate the antics of the Goodwins.

The success of the Salem girls far exceeded their intentions. Certainly their success led to imitations, for at least one wise father took to a remote part of his house his eighteen-year-old daughter and there " trounced her soundly " until she confessed that her afflictions and accusations were the result of a desire to obtain the notoriety of Ann Putnam and Abigail Williams, two of the most heavily afflicted and most willingly accusing of the Salem girls.

For the Salem hysteria had its rise in a small gathering of young girls who met one evening a week to learn what magic a West-Indian slave woman could teach. Tituba and her husband, John Indian, were the servants of the Reverend Mr. Samuel Parris, the pastor of Salem Village church. Parris's nine-year-old daughter Elizabeth and his eleven-year-old niece Abigail Williams were the first afflicted children in Salem Village; and the niece, Abigail, remained in the limelight throughout the summer. Elizabeth, however, was sent away from Salem to the care of friends who told the child to call the devil a " lyar " when he appeared to her. This she did and he came to her no more. The removal of his own child is the one action of Mr. Parris's which it is difficult to explain away. He has been represented as villain enough to have planned out the whole campaign during which twenty people were executed, and large numbers lost freedom, property, and health, some even dying in prison from exposure and harsh treatment. It is questionable if even he could have foreseen the scope of the affair; and even more questionable that he deliberately planned it, unlovely as the part he played was — he was a witness against many if not most of the accused; he preached vehement sermons; he encouraged the afflicted children; and he complacently recorded the examinations of the victims. Parris's disputes over firewood and over the ownership of the parsonage land had been many and bitter. That he listened eagerly to accusations against those he did not like is more than probable; that he actively planned the course of accusations one finds hard to believe. Narrow and disagreeable though he was, one cannot readily attach to him such malignant maliciousness. It is more likely that as the afflicted girls fidgeted the thought came to him, " Can it perhaps be that this enemy of mine is also a witch? " To ask the girls was to get affirmation; a name once suggested to them was marked. And in this way Parris did direct them.

His own account is that these girls, varying in age from nine to twenty, two of them maidservants, learned magic from his Indian slave Tituba. The worthy Mr. Griggs, called to attend the children of the Parris household, being unable to diagnose their illness, said " Witchcraft! " Thereupon John Indian, following the advice of Sister Mary Sibly (who later made public confession in church), mixed a cake of oaten flour with the children's urine and fed it to the dog. Upon this the children began to accuse certain people of having afflicted them, and the devil was let loose.

In the person of a little black man the devil now stalked through the villages, sat on people's bedposts in the shape of some one of the accused, whispered in the accused's ears, and held a Witches' Sabbath in Mr. Parris's field. Meanwhile the afflicted children frothed at the mouth, vomited pins, threw their legs and arms and necks out of joint, were constantly pinched and bitten — they could always show the marks of the teeth of the accused of the moment, whether she were little five-year-old Dorcas Good or some toothless old person — and were most amazingly and ingeniously " tortored."

Into this turmoil, already two months old, stepped Governor Phips, returning to New England with Increase Mather and the new charter the middle of May. No one had as yet been executed, but at least one woman had died in jail. Several persons were awaiting trial, among them

THE WITCHCRAFT BILL

George Burroughs, formerly pastor of the Salem Village Church, graduate of Harvard, friendly enough to have dined seven years earlier with Samuel Sewall, who made one of the judges to try and condemn him. After the excitement was over Governor Phips, wishing to set his own part in the best possible light, wrote to England: ". . . att my arrivall here I found the Prisons full of people comitted upon suspicion of witchcraft & that continuall complaints were made to me that many persons were grievously tormented by witches & that they cryed out upon severall persons by name, as the cause of their torments the number of these complaints increasing every day, by advice of the Lieut. Govr. & the Councill I gave a Comission of Oyer and Terminer to try the suspected witches & *at that time* the generality of the people represented the matter to me as reall witchcraft & gave very strange instances of the same. The first in Comission was the Lieut. Govr. & the rest persons of the best prudence & figure that could then be pitched upon & I depended upon the Court for a right method of proceeding in cases of witchcraft; at that time I went to command the army at the Eastern part of the Province [*i.e.,* Maine] for the French and Indians had made an attack upon some of our Frontier Towns, I continued there for some time but *when I returned I found people much dissatisfied at the proceedings of the Court* for about Twenty persons were condemned & executed of which number *some* were *thought by many persons to be innocent."*

The governor's alibi need not be questioned as much as the legality of the court he established. However, such a court he seems, as a royal governor, to have had the power to establish when the general court was not sitting. This Court of Oyer and Terminer was composed of men who were in no sense lawyers. There was no adequate provision for the study of law in the colony, which was now in the main ruled by men of the second generation and not by men trained in England. Men were made judges by virtue of their native ability and sound reputation. Those constituting this Court of Oyer and Terminer were able and honest, one of them indeed so honest and able that he retired from the court almost immediately, expressing his dissatisfaction with its procedure. But the ablest man of all led in the persecution — the lieutenant governor, William Stoughton, Harvard 1650, who had been made a magistrate after he had successfully preached in England and had steadfastly refused to become assistant minister to Richard Mather. This man, thirty-two years Cotton Mather's senior, never wavered in his belief that these people were witches and that they had been righteously executed. It may be that his early theological training fostered his bigoted attitude. But history has never lacked judges who tried cases with foregone conclusions, to whom anyone accused was *ipso facto* guilty.

IV

These silly girls of Salem Village must have been flattered that they had not only focused the attention of the entire colony upon them, but that a special court of prominent men had been appointed to listen to them. Further encouraged by Parris and by neighboring ministers, especially Noyes and Hale, they proceeded to astonish their audiences with more and more weird performances and more and more ridiculous statements. As they listened the country folk would nod their heads and say: " I always did think So-and-so was a witch. I remember ten years ago my cow died queerly. Wasn't that the week Goody Good knocked at my door? " Five years ago a cart stuck in front of Goody Bishop's door; last week a pig died after its owner had refused to buy something from Goody This-or-that. One man saw a black thing jump in his window; " the Body was like that of a Monkey, the Feet like a Cocks, but the Face much like a man's "; it vanished; he looked out his door and saw Goody Bishop crossing her orchard. Obviously " It " was she.

The first accusations fell upon two rather friendless women. Goody Good was poor; she sometimes begged; she may have spoken evilly of those who refused her charity. Goody Bishop was a menace to the peace of the village; she wore a bodice with red on it; and she kept a sort of tavern where young men played shuffleboard, drank cider, and made much noise. When the girls saw yellow birds between the fingers of these women; when they saw Good and Bishop sitting on their bedposts, on fence rails, on beams in the courtroom ceiling, people were only too ready to cry, " Witch! " Drunk with success, the girls proceeded. They next accused worthy women of substance, women who had led kindly, pious lives, but who were readily arrested and convicted. At no time after the very first did they restrict themselves to the popular idea of a witch, for their victims later were not always either old or suspicious. At least two of the accused escaped death by pleading pregnancy; and even their earliest prisoner, Sarah Good, could not have been very ancient, since the five-year-old Dorcas or Dorrithy imprisoned and chained with her was not even her youngest child. She had indeed been suspected of having murdered a baby born later than Dorcas. She was a poor woman with an evil tongue; but she was hardly a " hagged old woman." Tituba, the slave, was also arrested at once; however, her full and interestingly detailed confessions kept her from the gallows.

Like his neighbors, Giles Corey went to hear all the gossip about witches and to see the afflicted girls perform. His wife Martha objected. She would not go herself; and she tried to prevent his going to the extent, rumor had it, of unsaddling his horse. Upon this the girls " cried out " upon her. But she was a church member in good standing, one whose piety and honorable position in the community were unquestioned. Two members of the church, young men of thirty-six and seven, thought it their " duty to goe to her and see what shee would say to this complaint " of one of the girls that she did often " tortor her by pinching and otherways." They " had a great deal of talke with her about the complaine that was of her, and how greatly the name of God and religion and the church was dishonored by this meanes, but shee seemed to be no ways concerned for any thing about it but only to stop the mouthes of people that they might not say thus of her, shee told us that shee did not thinke that there were any witches, wee told her we were fully satisfied about the first three that they were such persons they were accused for, shee said that if they were wee could not blame the devill for making witches of them, for they were idle sloathfull persons and minded nothing that was good. but we had no reason to thinke so of her, for shee had made a profession of Christ and rejoyced to go and hear the word of God. and the like. but wee told her it was not making an outward profession that would clear her from being a witch, for it had been often

[111]

so in the wourld that witches had crept into the churches. . . ."

Martha Corey paid for her incredulity with her life; and her husband, credulous until he was himself accused, suffered the terrible death of *peine forte et dure,* being pressed beneath heavy weights that slowly crushed life out while his jailers offered him one day a crust of mouldy bread, the next day a mouthful of stagnant water, alternating these unlovely offerings according to the law, and on their own initiative poking back his protruding tongue with a cane. This sentence was his because he remained " mute," refusing to plead guilty or innocent. The reasons for Giles Corey's refusal cannot be known. For a time it was held that he acted as he did in order to have the right to dispose of his property by will; but as other victims were not denied that right, and as such a motive is, after all, rather thin for the endurance of such torture as this slow crushing out of life, there must have been some deeper reason. Perhaps it is to be found in the very religion which permitted such things. Having at first listened to and acquiesced in the accusations against his wife, Giles Corey when he was himself accused, may have felt that by his more painful death he might in some measure atone for his lack of loyalty to her. He knew both his own innocence and his inability to prove it to a court ready to convict anyone. A truthful plea of not guilty would surely send him to the gallows. Like his wife and the others who were executed during the summer, he refused to save his life by the false plea of guilty. The twenty victims all sacrificed their lives rather than live through a lie; for in every case these people defended their innocence, knowing full well that a confession would save them. Some few did indeed confess, and then in shame retract their confession and die. Some, indeed, did save their lives by confession and the accusation of others — for no one who confessed to witchcraft was executed. The twenty who died were executed not for *being* witches, but for refusing to *admit* themselves witches. For Cotton Mather and for all who thought as he did this was the greatest proof of their guilt, that in the face of direct testimony they declared themselves innocent.

Bridget Bishop had been executed summarily early in June. Sarah Osburn had died in jail in May. Tituba was held in jail to be used as a witness. Sarah Good was hanged in July after more than four months' imprisonment. Lone executions were not so much of a spectacle — a warning the ministers would have phrased it — as multiple ones. To see " eight firebrands of hell " swinging at once was doubtless a sad but edifying sight. Two people, a man and a woman, were hanged on June 30th; four women on the 19th of July; three men and a woman on the 19th of August; and the " eight firebrands of hell " on the 22nd of September, four days after Giles Corey's sentence. There were, then, in all, six orgies of execution, including eighty-year-old Giles Corey's prolonged suffering. But the number of arrests, preliminary examinations, and trials was large. Governor Phips said that when he " put an end to the Court " of Oyer and Terminer " there were at least fifty persons in prison *in*

*great misery by reason of the extreme cold & their pov-
erty.*" This does not account for those already executed,
nor for those who escaped hanging by flight.

The governor was right in emphasizing the " great
misery " of the prisoners. Many of them were kept in jail
for months, dragged back and forth from Boston jail to
Salem courtroom, where they were peered at, snarled at,
and prayed over. They wore chains, as the records of
expenses showed; even little " Dorcas " or " Dorrithy "
or " Dorythy " Good, five years old, wore chains; but
there is one human record: " To 2 blankets for Sarah
Goods child." Such charity pales when it is remembered
that all expenses were charged to the prisoners; and even
after the governor's pardon those who could not pay
could not go free, Tituba the slave being sold for her
keep.

These prisoners were examined in the ruthless fashion
of witch-finding. They were kept awake for long hours
and cunningly questioned — much like our present-day
victims of the third degree. They were minutely examined by a jury of their own sex and perhaps a doctor, for
" diabolical teats." To sensitive, well-bred, delicate
women to whom modesty was a very real virtue this
searching was a greater ordeal than that of the crowded
courtroom.

The trial scenes were even more entertaining than our
modern divorce and murder trials. The accused were
properly badgered; they were made to avert their eyes
and touch the afflicted girls, who thereupon recovered
from the tantrum of the moment. Bold John Alden asked

[114]

why, if the look of the accused was so virulent, the judge was not afflicted when they looked at him? All sorts of admissions were wrung from the prisoners; one "denyed" that his house was haunted, but admitted "there were toads." Some were so far goaded as to confess their guilt and accuse others. In their terror they were willing to admit anything that might save them. One girl having confessed and accused her already imprisoned grandfather, vainly retracted her confession, begging his pardon humbly. The confessions were eagerly heard; and the more details given of Satan, his ways and wiles, and the habits and horrors of witches, the happier the audience. They could feel that they were sharing in forbidden knowledge, playing with fire without scorching their fingers.

v

As time went on the afflicted girls became more skilled, providing more varied amusement to the bystanders. These girls constantly gave their sworn testimony that apparitions in the likeness of the accused came to them and "tortured" them by choking, pinching, pricking with pins, and the like. This is the so-called specter evidence upon which the justice of the trials finally hinged. It was a matter of very grave concern whether or not the devil could impersonate an innocent person. In general it was felt that he could not; and therefore if the specter of a person was seen, that person must be in league with the devil. "Pure specter evidence" needed, some thought, something to add to its weight. Usually there were plenty of people ready to

[115]

come forward with a tale of a bewitched cow, or a wagon-load of wood or supplies stuck in front of the accused's house, or the death of a pig after its owner had refused a favor to the accused.

In June, after the execution of Bridget Bishop, the ministers of Boston gave, at the request of the governor and council, their opinion on the witchcraft trials. In this document they stated the " need of a very critical and exquisite Caution, lest by too much Credulity for things received only upon the Devil's Authority, there be a Door opened for a long Train of miserable Consequences, and Satan get an advantage over us. . . ." Except for the statement that at the " first Enquiry " of a suspected person there should be " as little as is possible, of such Noise, Company, and Openness, as may too hastily expose them that are examined " there is no expression of the danger to the *accused*. Specter evidence they considered not in itself sufficient, " inasmuch as 'tis an undoubted and a notorious thing, that a Daemon may, by God's permission, appear even to ill purposes, in the Shape of an innocent, yea, and a vertuous Man." This advice of the minister's was drawn up by Cotton Mather. Furthermore, he had on May 31st written to John Richards, one of his friends, a judge of the Court of Oyer and Terminer: ". . . And yet I must most humbly beg you that in the Management of the affair . . . you do not lay more stress upon pure Spectre testimony then it will bear. When you are satisfyed or haue good plaine legall Evidence that the Daemons which molest our poore neighbours, do indeed represent such & such people to the

[116]

sufferers, thô this be a presumption, yet I suppose you will not reckon it a conviction that the people so represented are witches to be imediately exterminated. It is very certain that the divells haue sometimes represented the shapes of persons not onely innocent, but also very vertuous. Thô I believe that the juſt God then ordinarily provides a way for the Speedy vindications of the persons thus abused. Moreover I do suspect that persons who haue too much indulged themselves in Malignant, Envious, malicious Ebullitions of their soules, may unhappily expose themselves to the Judgment of being represented by Divels; of whom they never had any vision, & with whom they haue much lesse written any Covenant. I would say this; If upon the bear supposeall of a poore creatures being represented by a Spectre, too great a progresse be made by the Authority in ruining a poor neighbour so represented, it may be that a doore may be thereby openned for the Divils to obteine from the Courts in the invisible world a license to proceed unto moſt hideous desolations upon the repute & repose of such as haue yet been kept from the great transgression."

The governor in his letter to England ſtated that " Mr. Increase Mather & severall other Divines did give it as their Judgment that the Devill might afflict in the shape of an innocent person." But it was comparatively simple to find the further evidence the miniſters required, according to " such Judicious Writers as *Perkins* and *Bernard*," evidence, for example, that " Men of *Honeſty* and *Credit* " report some one to be a witch. In Salem Village, once a person was accused, more than one apparently

[117]

honest farmer would lay to his or her door misfortunes to his stock, his crop, his barns. Perkins gives other proofs resting upon air as thin as this. And he, like some modern judges, laid great stress upon consciousness of guilt: *" If the party examined be Unconstant, or contrary to himself, in his deliberate Answers, it argueth a Guilty Conscience, which stops the freedom of Utterance. And yet there are causes of Astonishment, which may befal the Good, as well as the Bad."*

But the judges paid less attention to the warnings of the clergymen than to their concluding statement: " Nevertheless, We cannot but humbly recommend unto the Government, the speedy and vigorous Prosecution of such as have rendred themselves obnoxious, according to the Direction given in the Laws of God, and the wholesome Statutes of the *English* Nation, for the Detection of Witchcrafts." Now the " law of God " was " thou shalt not suffer a witch to live," and such was the interpretation the judges put upon the advice of the ministers.

Speedy and vigorous was their prosecution. The afflicted girls had only to mention a man or woman to cause arrest and to find ready a host of witnesses eager to swear that they had been " tortored " by the accused's apparition. " You tax me for a wizard," shouted one stout old man. " You might as well tax me for a buzzard! " " I am no more a witch than you are a wizard," stormed Goody Good to her persecutor, the Reverend Mr. Noyes, " and if you hang me God will give you blood to drink! " Of this picturesque threat and its ful-

fillment when, years later, Noyes died of apoplexy, Haw-
thorne makes use in *The House of the Seven Gables*.

The attitude of the judges is clear from the case of
Rebecca Nurse, a gentle invalid, who was first declared
not guilty. But the Court, choosing to misinterpret a
simple statement of hers, speedily reversed the verdict.
She was hanged with four others in July.

It was in August that the Reverend George Burroughs
was hanged, that wiry little minister, once of Salem Village, whose exploits of physical strength seemed to an
age far from athletic to prove his league with the devil.
Burroughs, Harvard graduate, quondam guest of that
very Sewall who now made one of his judges, was " Accused by Eight of the Confessing Witches, as being an
head Actor at some of their Hellish Randezvouzes."
There had, it seems, been a Witches' Sabbath in the
Reverend Mr. Parris's field; and here all the confessing
witches saw Burroughs standing as the vice-regent of
Hell. He brought the devil's book to various women to
sign. One witness testified that in a trance she had been
carried by Burroughs " into a very high Mountain, where
he shewed her mighty and glorious Kingdoms, and said,
*He would give them all to her, if she would write in his
Book;* but she told him, *They were none of his to give;*
and refused the Motions; enduring much Misery for that
refusal." All the necks of the large audience must have
been craned to catch sight of anyone so virtuous as this
witness. Her testimony was undoubted. Burroughs himself could not explain it nor could he explain why the
devil was so unwilling to have testimony recited against

Burroughs — the afflicted girls were in terrible torment during his trial. Burroughs desperately trying to bring reason into court " pull'd out of his Pocket a Leaf that he had got of Mr. *Ady's* Book to prove that the Scripture Witchcrafts were not like ours," but " that Defence was not able to save him." Ady had published in London in 1656 *A Candle in the Dark or a Treatise concerning the Nature of Witches and Witchcraft* and in 1661 *A Perfect Discovery of Witches.* People, however, were more ready to believe writers like Perkins and Glanvil who merely persuaded them that their own views were right; and told them more horrors than they could think up for themselves.

Samuel Sewall, one of the judges, writing in the margin, " Dolefull Witchcraft! " made this entry in his diary: " This day George Burrough, John Willard, Jno. Procter, Martha Carrier and George Jacobs were executed at Salem, a very great number of spectators being present. Mr. Cotton Mather was there, Mr. Sims, Hale, Noyes, Chiever &c. All of them said they were iñocent, Carrier and all. Mr. Mather says they all died by a Righteous Sentence. Mr. Burrough by his Speech, Prayer, protestation of his Innocence, did much move unthinking persons, which occasions their speaking hardly concerning his being executed." The " Mr. Mather " has often been supposed to refer to Cotton Mather, but as Sewall always refers to him as " Mr. Cotton Mather " or " Mr. Mather the younger," it was probably Increase who thus upheld the sentence.

Cotton Mather's feelings on the guilt of the Reverend

Mr. Burroughs were expressed in a letter written shortly before his execution, a letter which is, however, far more interested in a recent earthquake at Jamaica than in witchcraft, of which it says: " Our Good God is working of Miracles. Five Witches were Lately Executed, impudently demanding of God, a Miraculous Vindication of their Innocency. Immediately upon this, Our God Miraculously sent in Five Andover-Witches, who made a most ample, surprising, amazing Confession, of all their Villainies and declared the Five newly executed to have been of their Company; discovering many more; but all agreeing in Burroughs being their Ringleader, who, I suppose, this Day receives his Trial at Salem, whither a Vast Concourse of people is gone; My Father, this morning among the rest. Since those, there have come in other Confessors; yea, they come in daily. About this prodigious matter my Soul has been Refreshed with some Little short of Miraculous Answers of prayer; which are not to bee written; but they comfort mee with a prospect of an hopeful Issue."

It is easy to see why suspicious characters preferred to become confessors before accusation attached to them. There was, aside from a desire for personal safety, a desire to share in the excitement as a participator, an actor of at least secondary importance to the afflicted girls. Had there been newspapers their headlines would have rioted in the details of diableries confessed by these self-declared witches.

It is not so easy to see why Cotton Mather did not, like his father, attend the trials; unless it was simply that he lacked the time. His parish work was heavy; and his outside activities many. He it was who visited the prisoners constantly, praying with and for them, and trying to lead their souls to God. A repentant witch might be saved; one who refused to confess was indubitably damned. Obstinate Martha Carrier was, therefore, a " rampant hag," " Queen of Hell."

Most of the women accused, though not necessarily poor, were still of the class referred to as " Goody," Mrs. being reserved for gentlefolk. Burroughs was, of course, a gentleman; and seventy-year-old John Alden was a captain, who did not inherit his father's hesitance of spirit. Committed to prison without bail, he endured confinement for fifteen weeks, " and then observing the manner of Tryals, and Evidence then taken, was at length prevailed with to make his Escape," returning the following spring when, none appearing against him, he was cleared by the Superior Court.

Mrs. Cary, a delicately bred lady, was arrested and kept in prison with eight-pound irons on her legs. At her preliminary examination, according to her husband's indignant account, " she was forced to stand with her Arms stretched out. I did request that I might hold one of her hands, but it was denied me; then she desired me to wipe the Tears from her Eyes, and the Sweat from her Face, which I did; then she desired she might lean herself on me, saying, she should faint.

" *Justice Hathorn* replied, she had strength enough to torment those persons, and she should have strength enough to stand." Mr. Cary visited the trials, and seeing that " the same Evidence that served for one, would serve for all the rest," effected her escape to Rhode Island and thence, to evade pursuit, to New York, whose Governor was hospitable to fugitives from Massachusetts witch-baitings.

He it was who received Philip English and his wife, wealthy people of consequence who had been lodged in Boston jail but given their liberty during the day. On the day before that set for their trial at Salem the two ministers of the Old South Church invited them to services — English is supposed to have been an Episcopalian. These ministers, Willard and Moodey, were not in sympathy with the witchcraft investigations. On this Sunday Mr. Moodey preached, taking for his text, " If they persecute you in one city, flee to another." Afterwards Mr. Moodey paid a visit to the Englishes, inquiring if they understood his import. English was inclined to rely upon God's help to prove their innocence, but his wife said, " Do you not think that they, who have suffered already, are innocent? " Mr. Moodey then said that if English did not care to move, he himself would send Mrs. English to a place of safety. Mrs. English had been confined for six weeks in Salem jail, and then had been removed to Boston, where her husband, for his close attention and devotion to her, was also arrested. It was toward the end of April that she was first accused. So it was in the time of greatest excitement that she and her husband were taken to New York in a " Conveyance " provided by " several worthy Persons in Boston." They took with them letters from Governor Phips of Massachusetts to

[123]

Governor Fletcher of New York; all details of the journey had been carefully arranged; and Mr. Moodey had previously acquainted the Governor of New York so that he with several gentlemen was at hand to welcome the Englishes. Governor Phips does not mention this when he writes to England that he was off on a campaign in Maine during the witchcraft summer!

VI

Moodey, then, came out in the open in opposition to the general opinion of both leaders and masses. His fellow minister, Willard, moved more cautiously. He published a protest during the trials, but the publication was anonymous. This was a *Dialogue of S. and B.* (Salem and Boston?) arguing for reflection and for more sane procedure: ". . . reason tells us that the more horrible the Crime is, the more Cautious we ought to be in making any guilty of it." If God moves slowly in this matter of apprehending witches, he argued, who are we to hurry Him? Willard was accused by one of the Salem girls, who, however, was immediately reprimanded by the judge and told that she must mean one John Willard already in prison, a less prominent man. Thomas Brattle, who clearly saw the fault of the whole sad hysteria, did not, like Moodey and Willard, express his opinion freely. It was not until October, when the bubble of persecution had already burst, that he wrote his well-known letter, a letter written in answer to a direct query and not given to the public, but privately circulated among safe friends. Even then Brattle dared not sign it with more than his initials. In spite of its sanity this letter can bring him little credit, since it had nothing to do with stemming the tide of tragic absurdity. Brattle was not brave enough to risk his life — if indeed he would have risked it.

Nathaniel Saltonstall had voiced his protest in the very beginning by refusing to remain on the Court of Oyer and Terminer. Others of less consequence also spoke up sharply. Captain Joseph Putnam for weeks kept a horse saddled, ready to flee if he should be accused because of his known opposition to the proceedings. Thomas Wilkins, John Tarbell, and Samuel Nurse were excommunicated from the church because of their efforts to stop the trials. John Procter went to take his " jade " (maidservant) home from one of the girls' meetings and said she should be whipt. He paid for this with his life. William Rayment sharply told an afflicted girl " she lyed and the garl said she did it for sport they must have some sport." Francis Dane Senior of Andover petitioned for an accused woman, " I believe the reports haue been Scandalous and unjust neither will bear the light . . . and had Charity been put on the Diuel would not haue had such an advantage against us and I beleeve many Innocent persons have been accused. . . ." Petitions for prisoners were signed by many — one bears ninety-three signatures, of which twenty-four add " and his wyfe." John Wise, pastor of Ipswich, later strongly inimical to Cotton Mather, signed a petition for John Procter and his wife.

These pleas from neighbours of prisoners and from the accused themselves had often great dignity and power.

Rebecca Nurse petitioned the Judges " for my Life Lyes now in your Hands, under God: And being conscious of my owne Innocency. I humbly begg that I may haue liberty to manifeſt it. . . . And your Poore pettiſſioner shall Evermore pray as in duty bound." Even more moving is this plea from Ann Pudeator who tried to show that the evidence againſt her was " altogether false and untrue, and besides the aboveſaid Jno Beſt hath been formerly whipt, and likewise is recorded for A Lyar, I would humbly begg of your honours to Take it into your Judicious and Pious consideration, That my life may not be taken away by such false Evidences and witnesses as these. . . ." Mary Eaſty, already sentenced to die, petitioned the judges and " the Reverend Miniſters " not for her own life, " for I know I muſt die, and my appointed Time is set," but that " no more Innocent blood may be shed which undoubtedly cannot be avoyded In the way and course you goe in I queſtion not but your honours does to the utmoſt of your Power in the discouery . . . of witchcraft . . . and would not be guilty of Innocent blood for the world but by my own Innocencye I know you are in the wrong way the Lord in his infinite mercye direct you."

But very few of God's servants had any doubts about witchcraft. As miniſters it was their duty rather to seek out and help convict the children of Satan. At the very ſtart in the spring the Reverend Deodat Lawson contributed to the inflammation of men's minds by a passionate sermon in Salem Village. Noyes, Hale, Parris added fervid sermons. Cotton Mather lived in a ſtate of feverish excitement. He was not yet thirty and had already attained great prominence. His opinion was of weight. He felt it necessary to study all possible authorities as well as

HANDWRITING OF COTTON MATHER

the cases in hand. He prayed to be " *altogether delivered from* Enchantments; *that no* Enchantment *on my Mind, may hinder mee from seeing or doing any thing for the*

Glory of God, or dispose mee to any thing whereat God may be displeased. The Reason of this Wish is, because I beleeve that a real and proper *Enchantment,* of the *Divels,* do's *blind,* and *move* the Minds of the moſt of Men; even in Inſtances of every sort. But I remember, that much *Faſting* as well as *Prayer,* is necessary, to obtain a Rescue from *Enchantment."* He offered to take any six of the afflicted girls into his own house and try to effect their cure — as he had successfully done with the oldeſt Goodwin child — by faſting and prayer. He demonſtrated the efficacy of this method with two later cases, Mercy Short and Margaret Rule.

But he did believe that the devil was abroad; that the accused were his agents; and that something draſtic ought to be done, ". . . at such a time as this ought *Magiſtrates* to do something *extraordinary* . . . in reſtraining and chaſtising of *Evil Doers."* He thanked God for the success " *given unto the Sedulous and Assiduous endeavours of our Honourable Rulers, to detect the abominable Witchcrafts."* He saw " in moſt of the *Judges,* a moſt charming Inſtance of *Prudence* and *Patience,* and I knew their exemplary *Pietie,* and the *Agony* of Soul with which they sought the Direction of Heaven; above moſt other People, whom I generally saw enchanted into a raging, railing, scandalous and unreasonable Disposition, as the Diſtress increased upon us: For this Cause tho' I could not allow the *Principles,* that some of the Judges had espoused, yett I could not but speak honourably of their *Persons,* on all occasions; and my *Compassion,* upon the Sight of their *Difficulties,*

[128]

raised by my Journeys to *Salem,* the chief Seat of these diabolical Vexations, caused mee yett more to do so."

This was written after the Court of Oyer and Terminer had been dissolved by Governor Phips. Phips wrote: " When I enquired into the matter I was enformed by the Judges that they begun with this [specter testimony] but had human testimony against such as were condemned & undoubted proof of their being witches, but at length I found that the Devill did take upon him the shape of innocent persons & some were accused of whose innocency I was well assured & *many considerable persons* of unblameable life & conversation were cried out upon as witches & wizards *the Deputy Gov*^r. notwithstanding *persisted vigorously in the same method to the great dissatisfaction & disturbance of the people* untill I put an end to the Court & stopped the proceedings . . . this delusion of the Devill did spread & its dismall effects touched the lives & estates of many of their Majesties Subjects & the reputacon of *some of the principall persons* here." Thus the end came when the afflicted girls, drunk with success and attention, struck at those dear to the men in power.

VII

There were many, however, who agreed with Cotton Mather that such an abrupt end might injure God and help the devil. A year later one Mrs. Carver of Salem told Mather " That a *new Storm* of *Witchcraft* would fall upon the Countrey; to chastise the Iniquity that was used in the wilful Smothering and Covering of the Last; and that many fierce Opposites to the discovery of that *Witch-craft* would be thereby convinced."

Stoughton, the lieutenant governor and chief justice of the court, did not confine his disapproval to an entry in a diary. With spectral evidence eliminated, the Superior Court on January 3rd, with Stoughton as chief justice, tried fifty-two people, of whom all were cleared " saving three," wrote Governor Phips, " & *I was enformed by the Kings Attorny Generall that some of the cleared and the condemned were under the same circumstances* or that there was the same reason to clear the three condemned as the rest according to his Judgment. The Deputy Govr. signed a Warrant for their speedy execucon & also of five others who were condemned at the former Court of Oyer and Terminer but considering how the matter had been managed I sent a reprieve whereby the execucon was stopped . . . *the Lieut. Govr. upon this occasion was inraged & filled with passionate anger & refused to sitt upon the bench in a Superior Court then held at Charles Towne & indeed hath from the beginning hurried on these matters with great precipitancy & by his warrant hath caused the estates, goods & chattles of the executed to be seized & disposed of. . . .*" To Stoughton the task of persecution was sweet. He believed not only that the accused were witches, but that he himself was doing God's work in trying to rid the country of the emissaries of Satan.

It is odd, in the public revulsion of feeling, that Stoughton went unscathed. His popularity was unharmed, and he retained not only office but complete public confidence to the day of his death. Upon the head of Parris, pastor of Salem Village, fell troubles aplenty. He had never managed to swing clear of disputes with his parishioners, who now, instead of feeling grateful for the theatrical series of tragedies, finally hounded him out of town. Parris considered himself rebuked by Divine Providence, since the outbreak started in his family and since his servants, though unknown to him, used diabolical means " to raise Spirits." " And by all, I do humbly own . . . before the Lord and his People that God has been righteously spitting in my face, Numb. xii. 14. And I desire to lie low under all this reproach, and to lay my hand on my mouth."

Cotton Mather at the close of the affair stood as high as ever in the public mind. For so young a man he had conducted himself with dignity. He had upheld the judges and he had been busy in the whole matter, constantly visiting the accused. His was not one of those minds that leap into the future at all times; in certain matters he did show himself far ahead of his times. But in this of witchcraft he stood solid with his father and most of the men and ministers of the day. There *were* witches; there *was* a Devil; there *were* afflicted people. And seemingly the surest way to relieve the afflicted, to discourage the devil, and to glorify God was to exterminate the witches. It is idle to blame a man for not being ahead of his generation.

But it is fair to blame him for not making a serious study of both sides of the question. With his mental ability he ought to have been able to see that there was another side. Nevertheless, he ſtands head and shoulders above such men as Thomas Brattle, who, seeing the light, dared not hold it aloft. Thomas Brattle, as his letter amply proves, saw clearly that these people were innocent; that the whole matter was a delusion. Yet he did not lift up his voice and attempt to ſtay the executions. Lesser men and women gave up their lives because they declared that there were no witches. Brattle saved his life; and then when all was safe came out in ſtrong measure againſt the delusion — and againſt Cotton Mather toward whom he had been inimical even in college days. The reading of Brattle's letter can but awaken indignation that, seeing the truth, he did not have the courage to proclaim it aloud. And when years later he uses his clear vision in order to blacken Mather's character, hiding himself be-hind another man's name, he appears pitiful indeed. A wise man, a prominent man, he let others suffer and die without risking anything to save them.

Cotton Mather, his persecution mania revived, noted in his diary that people later reviled him as if he " had been the Doer of all the hard Things, that were done, in the Prosecution of the *Witchcraft*." Sensitive as he always was, he felt aspersions keenly and doubtless took to himself many that were meant for others. Some scapegoat was obviously needed; and the Brattles, per-haps to defend their own silence, chose to promote a feeling of censure toward their enemies, the Mathers. By throwing sufficient mud at others they could hide their own laodicean policy. Not that there was attempt made to vilify them. The people were heartily sick of the matter. Most of them had been such eager listeners, if not actual participants, of the tragic nonsense that very shame forced them to silence. When the tide started to turn, people in general were terrified into quiet; Cotton Mather continued to state the truth as he saw it. Mather and Stoughton were on the wrong side, but at least they were honest in their being there; they were right in that they acted entirely according to their strongest convictions. They followed the light as they saw it. Mather remained an honored preacher, much sought after, especially in Salem, where he preached constantly in the following year, and frequently in all the years to come. He was among the ministers called in to settle Parris's further difficulties with his parish. Until the Brattles stirred up a hornet's nest of gossip he could rest serene, troubled only by the fear that the devil had not been sufficiently chastised.

It was never his practice to hide his light under a bushel. He held it aloft for the world to see. It was his misfortune that this time his light was darkness.

CHAPTER FIVE

*"Herein I would propose . . to have my Body
more notably made a Temple of God . ."*
— *Diary of Cotton Mather*

I

WHEN the witchcraft trials ended in 1693 God had been upheld, the devil had been shamed, and all was right with the Mathers. Nine years later their political power was gone. After 1702 no Mather would ever again ſtand before kings, make and unmake magiſtrates, and be as the elders in the old days of independence.

The root of these nine troubled years of defeat lay in Increase's agency in England. Associated with him had been Elisha Cooke, who had violently opposed the acceptance of the new charter in 1691. The new charter represented a new order, a liberal franchise, and the downfall of the theocratic oligarchy. Politically, then, Increase and Cotton Mather represented liberalism. But Cooke never forgave his fellow agent for making off with all the glory. Immediately upon his return to Massachusetts Cooke began to ſtir up dissatisfaction. When he was refused membership in the Council by Governor Phips in 1693 his rage fell upon Increase Mather as the power behind the throne. From that time Cooke represented the party who were all for the good old times of

[134]

the founders of the colony, when a charter was a real charter — and might still have been were it not for the power-drugged Increase Mather, who was all for the king by whom he had been received, and who had no good words for the real representatives of the real people.

Had Cooke been the Mathers' only enemy, he could have done little beyond causing Cotton's outbreak in 1693 against " the cursed *Reproches* with which this unworthy, ungodly, ungrateful People, do load not myself only, but both of my *Fathers* too."

But if the Mathers were of the liberal party in politics, they were of the conservative party in religion. When, therefore, in 1699 a group of men, dissatisfied with the rigor of the old Congregationalism, proposed a new " Church in Brattle Square " to be organized according to a manifesto, which they published, wherein they asserted that they " dared not refuse baptism to any child offered by any professed Christian, upon his engagement to see it educated . . . in the Christian religion . . ." whether or not the parents were church members; that no relations of religious experiences would be required of those who partook of the Holy Sacrament (the Mathers' church had required public profession at first before the entire congregation, later before a smaller group of elders); and finally that " we cannot confine the right of choosing a minister to communicants alone; but we think that every baptized adult person, who contributed to the maintenance, should have a vote in electing "; when these things were announced Cotton Mather's temper exploded. " A Company of Head-strong

Men in the Town," he cried, " the cheef of whom, are full
of malignity to the Holy Wayes of our Churches, have
built in this Town, another Meeting-house." They are
" fallacious people "; their manifesto will " utterly sub-
vert our Churches "; they are moved by " vilent and
impetuous Lusts "; they are led by Satan.

The call of God to battle rings in Cotton Mather's ears.
Such a devil's company " drives the Ministers, that would
bee faithful unto the Lord Jesus Christ, and His Interests
in the Churches, into a Necessity of appearing for their
Defence. No little Part of these Actions must unavoidably
fall to my Share." The struggle had come providentially.
Only a few months before he had been smitten with the
favor that God had shown to him though he was " such
an horribly guilty and filthy Sinner, (in some Respects,
above any that I know, of my Generation); and yett my
Sin, employ'd in more than ordinary Service, for the
Churches of my Lord Jesus Christ." A short time before
that he had lamented his " horrible Filthiness, Unthank-
fulness, and Unfruitfulness. . . . And now my Mind is
horribly buffeted with *Temptations,* which tell mee, that
being unable to do any further Service, and unworthy
that God should help mee to do any, I shall fall into an
unserviceable old-Age, before I am forty years old." Now
with this open onslaught against true Christianity his
work was cut out for him, and both he and his father
rushed to the charge. They were not alone. The entire
conservative clergy joined forces against the new church
and its young pastor, Benjamin Colman, a Harvard
graduate ordained in England, and chosen by that same

[136]

Brattle who had been at odds with Cotton Mather since their Harvard days. The founders of this church were bent upon their iniquity and the future of Congregationalism had to take its chances. Only a few months after the formation of the Brattle Street Church Cotton Mather finds " the *Innovators,* that have sett up a *new Church* in *Boston* . . . ignorant, arrogant, obstinate, and full of Malice and Slander. and they fill the Land with *Lyes,* in the Misrepresentation whereof, I am a very singular Sufferer."

A call to the service of God in helping the First Church had, in the meantime, been no more successful. He had looked about him for work to do which would " bee a Thing acceptable to Heaven, . . . and a Demonstration of Sincerity, in my Dispositions to the Interests of my Lord Jesus Christ. . . ." So he decided that the old First Church needed something to stir up its slothful members; perhaps a better minister, one " of some *Age,* and great Ability, and Authority, and Experience, and of eminent Piety, and of a peaceable Temper, and of Congregational principles, and a popular and plausible preacher." Such a paragon he knew in West Jersey. Forthwith he suggested his name to the leaders of the First Church, who up to now had somehow managed to direct their own affairs and choose their own ministers. To facilitate the matter Cotton Mather offered himself to open up correspondence with the paragon. But when " the young Man, their present pastor " heard how far the matter had gone, he was most ungrateful; he turned bitterly upon Cotton Mather " and stirr'd up a Storm of most unworthy *Reproaches*." This was the reward of his " sincere and Zelous Labours," a new crop of enemies.

The Brattle Street Church went on its way in spite of opposition, and in the end Cotton Mather helped to draw up an agreement whereby all four churches in Boston could live in harmony. This was his policy all through life; when the things he opposed could not be overthrown, he turned his efforts toward making them useful; at worst he could thus mitigate their harm; at best who knows what he with the help of the Lord could in time accomplish? Hence in January, 1700, the New Church was instituted and " Mr. Colman reads the Writing agreed on." " Mr. Willard pray'd God to pardon all the frailties and follies of Ministers and people; and that they might give that Respect to the other churches that was due to them though were not just of their Constitution. Mr. Mather in's Sermon, and Mr. Cotton Mather in's prayer to the same purpose. Mr. Willard and C. Mather pray'd excellently and pathetically for Mr. Colman and his Flock. Twas a close dark day." Mr. Colman lived to be a bearer at Cotton Mather's funeral and to preach his eulogy, but the less saintly of the flock never forgave the Mathers. In this distinguished congregation at the opening of the new church was saturnine Elisha Cooke, whom no prayers, however " pathetical," could have moved from his implacable hatred.

But the real fight in which the Mathers found themselves in these critical years concerned Harvard College rather than politics or religion. When Increase Mather was serving the colony in England, he was president of

Harvard as well as pastor of the North Church. In his church Cotton watched over his interests; the government and instruction of the college devolved upon two young tutors, John Leverett and William Brattle, who were later to oust the Mathers forever from Harvard. In 1692 one act of Governor Phips and his council was to grant Harvard a charter. Since the fall of the colony charter, and with it Harvard's charter, there had been no provision for the college. It had merely continued to function as before. Now under Phips's provision the new corporation speedily conferred upon President Mather the degree of Doctor of Divinity, and upon Brattle and Leverett the degree of Bachelor of Divinity. The king soon vetoed the charter granting such privileges, but the degrees remained as conferred. Both Brattle and Leverett favored the new Brattle Street Church, of which Brattle's brother Thomas was one of the instigators; and both urged Colman to become its minister. This was enough to bring them into conflict with the president. Being opposed by Increase Mather meant that they were immediately welcomed as friends by Elisha Cooke and his conservative anti-Mather party in the House of Delegates, the popular branch of the General Court.

With the vetoing of the college charter in 1692 by the king it became clear that the task of securing a charter would be most difficult if the college were to continue under the direction of the old Congregational rule so stoutly defended by its president. Increase Mather felt that were he permitted to go to England once more as an agent he could secure a satisfactory charter. So sure was he that he began to realize that it was God rather than his own desires who had suggested the plan. This divine assurance he communicated to Cotton, who was moved to pray about the matter. All things both great and small were with these men and, indeed with most of their contemporaries, submitted to God in fervent prayer. Even more worldly men such as Sewall felt that God directly assured them at times that their prayers were to be granted. So in June, 1699, Cotton Mather might well feel: ". . . this Day, as I was, (may I not say?) in the Spirit, it was in a powerful Manner assured mee from Heaven, that my Father shall one Day be carried unto England: and that he shall there glorify the Lord Jesus Christ: and that the *Particular Faith* which had introduced it, shall be at last made a matter of wonderful Glory and Service unto the Lord.

" And thou; *O Mather* the Younger, shalt live to see this accomplished."

But the prophecy was in vain. Though Cotton Mather prayed and prostrated himself, though he and his father made drafts of new charters, though in June, 1700, he " went unto the house of Representatives, and made a Speech unto them, relating to the Methods of procuring a Settlement for the *Colledge* which is now languishing," and though the speech " found much Acceptance, and was of no little Consequence," yet a few days later he realized that all was lost. He had pleaded with God, he had fasted and prayed, but in the end Elisha Cooke in the House of Representatives and the men of the Brattle Street Church (who had been violently attacked by the

Mathers) and Leverett and Brattle (whom the Mathers had left out of their slate for the Corporation in their drafts of the charter) had prevailed. The " base unhandsomeness " of the governor, the " great Ebullitions of unaccountable Prœjudice, and Ingratitude " of the lieutenant governor, had been added to wickedness, chicanery, and open hostility. To Cotton Mather the whole affair was incomprehensible.

In August, 1701, Increase Mather resigned as president of Harvard; with his resignation ended his public life.

II

But before this the enemies of the Mathers had not scrupled to hunt up ways and means of villifying them. The witchcraft excitement had subsided soon after the governor's sweeping pardon; back to their homes went the frightened surviving victims, though some lingered in jail, unable to pay their prison fees. In time Philip English and his wife could safely return and claim recompense for their heavy financial losses. Public opinion, divided during the crisis, united in forgetfulness. To the mass of people it became merely an event of the past; newer affairs blotted it out. In the minds of a few, however, it lingered — for Cotton Mather the incident was never closed. Nineteen years later he still wondered what it was all about: " I entreated of the Lord, that I might understand the Meaning of the Descent from the Invisible World, . . . nineteen years ago." In the fall of 1696 The Reverend Mr. Willard " Spake smartly about the Salem Witchcrafts, and that no order had been suffer'd to come forth by Authority to ask God's pardon." That year, the day before Christmas, while his baby daughter lay dead in the house, Judge Sewall was moved by the Scriptures which his young son recited to him in Latin: "The 7th verse did awfully bring to mind the Salem Tragedie." (But if ye had known what this meaneth, I will have mercy and not sacrifice, ye would not have condemned the guiltless.) Because of this feeling on the part of the men who had honestly thought that they had acted in the best interests of God and man, those in authority came to believe that some public act was necessary to close the affair once and for all. Consequently, on the 14th of January, 1697, appointed by the General Court as a public fast day, prayers were said for "whatever might have been done amiss in the late tragedy, raised among us by Satan and his instruments, through the awful judgment of God." On the afternoon of this day Mr. Willard read to his congregation Judge Sewall's apology, Sewall "standing up at the reading of it, and bowing when finished":

"Samuel Sewall, sensible of the reiterated strokes of God upon himself and family; and being sensible, that as to the Guilt contracted upon the opening of the late Comission of Oyer and Terminer at Salem (to which the order for this Day relates) he is, upon many accounts, more concerned than any he knows of, Desires to take the Blame and shame of it, Asking pardon of men, And especially desiring prayers that God, who has an Unlimited Authority, would pardon that sin and all other his sins, personal and Relative: And according to his infinite

[142]

Benignity and Sovereignty, Not Visit the sin of him, or of any other, upon himself or any of his, nor upon the Land: But that He would powerfully defend him against all Temptations to Sin, for the future; and vouchsafe him the efficacious, saving Conduct of his Word and Spirit." Modern psychology would easily find in this traces of fear; Sewall apologized left God hew down more of his children with continued " reiterated Strokes."

For the public the matter was now completely closed. But Brattle, wily politician willing to use any means to undermine his enemies' power, the same man who in the fall of 1692 had written, but not published a letter, admirably controverting the mistaken views of the witch-persecutors, saw in this recantation of Sewall's a chance to attack the Mathers. Cotton Mather had not apologized. He had, indeed, nothing for which to apologize. He had acted according to the light as he saw it; and whereas his spirit was much perturbed by Sewall's action, he had sufficiently proved his own theories of the proper treatment of afflicted girls in 1693 in the cases of Mercy Short and Margaret Rule, for whose afflictions not one person had been even arrested as a witch. At the time of Sewall's confession of guilt Mather had written in his diary, first a list of all the shortcomings and vices of Massachusetts people, which he had publicly prayed against on the day of public fast; and then, as an afterthought: " Being afflicted last Night, with discouraging Thoughts as if unavoidable *Marks,* of the *Divine Displeasure* must overtake my *Family,* for my not appearing with *Vigor* enough to stop the proceedings of the Judges, when the Inextricable Storm from the *Invisible World* assaulted the Countrey, I did this morning, in prayer with my Family, putt my Family into the Merciful Hands of the Lord." Here was the hesitation of a man who tried always to act as God would have him; who, convinced of the reality of the descent of Satan, was not quite convinced that his own part in the affair had been properly played.

In June, 1698, he recorded: " There is a sort of Sadduccee in this Town; a man, who makes little Conscience of lying . . . [who] hath often abused mee. . . . I understand, that hee apprehends the shortest way to deliver People, from the *Beleef* of the Doctrines which not I only, but all the Ministers of Christ in the World, have hitherto mentioned, will bee, to show the World, what an *ill Man* I am." In this Cotton Mather shows much penetration. This man, who signed himself Robert Calfe or Calef, was the puppet of the Brattles. Mather was shrewd enough to see this. He recognized this as a move on the part of the " enemies of the Churches " who employed " one vile Tool, namely R. *Calf,*" to produce " filthy Scribbles, to hurt " Mather's " precious Opportunities of glorifying " the Lord. " E. P.," a contemporary who was no friend of the Mathers, wrote that Calef was " furnished with materials for his work by Mr. Brattle of Cambridge; and his brother, of Boston; and other gentlemen." Robert Calef was a Boston merchant, probably a weaver as well as a seller of cloth. Though he held certain minor offices such as that of tithing-man, assessor, and overseer of the poor, and though he was a man of substance, there is nothing to indicate that he was a man of learning. His one literary effort is this book published to discredit the Mathers. That this book betrays wide reading and considerable scholarship does not necessarily raise Calef to the rank of a scholar. Both Brattles were men of keen wit and wide learning. They might well have furnished more than the bare materials for the fight. They had no objection to underhand methods; and they knew that their blows would ring the louder for seeming to come from an unprejudiced hand. So with Calef as the author they published a book that utterly discredited both witchcraft and the Mathers, sending it to England since no Massachusetts press would print it. But it appeared for sale in the colony in 1700 and was eagerly bought by friends and enemies of the Mathers.

That the stand against witchcraft taken in this book is sane, enlightened, and modern does not excuse it. Had it been published or even attempted when the excitement was going on, when its publication might have stemmed the tide of fanaticism and saved innocent lives, no praise could have been sufficient for it or for its author and instigators. But neither Calef nor the Brattles came forth boldly then. There was no risk in 1698 or in 1700 long after Sewall had made confession and the public fast day had soothed the public conscience. In 1692 they were silent. Thomas Brattle's letter was written in the fall of 1692, but even then it was unsigned save by initials, and was circulated only among friends. Now that he wished to confound the Mathers he again forbore to come out into the open. Wishing to capitalize the subsidence of

[145]

the witchcraft mania and ſtir up revulsion especially
againſt those who were no friends of his, he and his
brother and their faction used Calef as their mouthpiece.
The attention he received from these men, both ariſto-
cratic and learned, muſt have been flattering to the merchant. He was not loath to accept the literary and social
honors his book brought. And there is no reason to believe
that he acted in anything but good faith, never sus-
pecting that these gentlemen were using him to their
own purpose.

Calef's book was particularly concerned with the case
of Margaret Rule, a young woman who was afflicted in
the fall of 1693. She was visited by both Mathers; but it
was Cotton who finally delivered her from her troubles
by faſting and prayer, having cautioned her againſt accusing anyone. Calef says that at this time he visited
Margaret Rule along with other curious people and can
therefore give an eye-witness's account of her gyrations.
He tells how Cotton Mather queſtioned the girl at length;
" Then he put his hand upon her Breaſt and Belly, *viz.*
on the Cloaths over her, and felt a Living thing, as he
said, which moved his Father also to feel, and some
others " (perhaps Mr. Calef, too?). In the book Calef
prints this account of his, together with the reply made
by Cotton Mather after he, Calef, had submitted it to him
before publication. Cotton Mather called it a false representation " That I rub'd Rule's Stomach, her Breaſt not
being covered. The Oath of the neareſt Spectators . . .
will prove this to be little less than a gross (if not a
doubled) Lie; and to be somewhat plainer, it carries the

[146]

Face of a Lie contrived on purpose (by them at least, to whom you are beholden for the Narrative) Wickedly and Basely to expose me. For you cannot but know how much this Representation hath contributed, to make People believe a Smutty thing of me. . . ."

Tradition based solely on the testimony of one man has it that Increase Mather, still president of Harvard, ordered the book burned in Harvard Yard. Cotton himself, though feeling this Calef a vile man, freely forgave him and in his prayers turned him over to God. The Mathers' parishioners were not, however, inclined to take the book calmly. After holding days of prayer they drew up an answer to this " Libellous Book lately come into this Countrey . . . which is writ (with what help we know not) by one Robert Calef."

III

After all, the book was but one more handful of mud to throw at the Mathers and lessen their power. In 1701 Increase Mather, who hitherto had managed the presidency of Harvard by two or three visits a week, was forced to move to Cambridge, where the climate did not, he thought, agree with him, where there was no suitable residence for him, and where the teaching of forty or fifty boys was small recompense for the loss of a congregation of fifteen hundred souls. That the compulsory residence was a device on the part of his enemies on the corporation to make him give up the office both he and his son were probably aware. If, however, they were ignorant they were soon enlightened after Increase's resignation when the new appointee was permitted to reside in Boston.

Wrath against the men who had brought about Increase's downfall boiled over in his son's heart. His father's enemies were his enemies; they were even worse, for he could forgive his own enemies. He burst out even against Sewall, who was always friendly with him. On October 20th, 1701, Sewall recorded: " Mr. Cotton Mather came to Mr. Wilkins's shop, and there talked very sharply against me as if I had used his father worse than a Neger; spake so loud that people in the street might hear him. Then went and told Sam, That one pleaded much for Negroes, and he had used his father worse than a Negro, and told him that was his father." Then the good judge remembered that on the 9th of October he had " sent Mr. Increase Mather a Hanch of very good Venison; I hope," he confides plaintively to his diary, " in that I did not treat him as a Negro."

Two days later Sewall was smarting under this attack and Cotton was boiling over. They met once more at the friendly bookshop of Mr. Wilkins, and Sewall " expostulated with him from 1 Tim., 5. 1. Rebuke not an elder. He said he had consider'd that: I told him of his book of the Law of Kindness for the Tongue, whether this were correspondent with that, Whether correspondent with Christ's Rule: He said, having spoken to me before there was no need to speak to me again; and so justified his reviling me behind my back. Charg'd the Council with Lying, Hypocrisy, Tricks, and I know not what all.

I ask'd him if it were done with that Meekness as it should; answer'd yes. Charg'd the Council in general, and then shew'd my share, which was my speech in Council. . . . I ask'd him If I should supõse he had done something amiss in his Church as an Officer; whether it would be well for me to exclaim againſt him in the ſtreet for it." By this time a crowd had collećted at the door to enjoy the quarrel and " Mr. Wilkin would fain have had him gon into the iñer room, but he would not." So off to the Council ſtalked the perturbed Sewall, leaving Cotton Mather in an unclerical rage. Sewall had his speech copied out and sent to the Mathers. The quarrel ended. But there are no more records of " hanches of venison."

A few years earlier Cotton Mather's enemies had been able to rejoice in the scandal that fell upon his family when his uncle John Cotton, son of the famous John Cotton, was dismissed from his church in Plymouth, though " with as much charity as the rule would permit." His dismissal came after his " Notorious Breaches of the Seventh Commandment, and undue Carriage in chusing Elders. Thus Chriſts words are fulfilled, Unsavoury Salt is caſt to the Dunghill," Sewall complacently recorded. But Cotton Mather was " under extreme Anguish of Mind." Though he admits the juſtice of the sentence, he can ſtill pity his " poor Uncle," with whom he remained on friendly terms and to whose widow he wrote consolingly when John Cotton speedily loſt his life of yellow feever after an expiating service as paſtor in Carolina. He held a faſt for the poor sinner; and also for himself "left the Lord should bring His dreadful Judgments upon *mee* also." It might be charity to ascribe to this uncle the tendencies of Cotton Mather's son Increase, that youth, who at birth in 1699 seemed to promise a special glorification of the Lord and whose subsequent career was a constant source of grief and mortification to his father.

IV

The life of Boston in these years had begun to broaden in scope and variety. The coming of royal governors brought to Boston varied and picturesque experiences such as it had never known in the days of chilly self-sufficiency. Some of the governors had been violent; all were picturesque. Sir William Phips in his short term "laid hands" upon the collector of the port and, after a quarrel with Captain Short of the *Nonesuch* frigate, the governor "made use of his cane and broke Short's head." Governor Bellomont, who succeeded Phips, was a "noble lord," in the Irish peerage, to be sure, but still a lord; and the savor of nobility was sweet in the nostrils of the codfish aristocracy. The legislature granted him more money than any other governor and were charmed with his courtesy and the grace of his lady. Judge Sewall basked in the warmth of her company. On a pleasant day in July, 1699, "I have my Lady up upon Cotton Hill, and shew her the Town; . . . Mrs. Tuthill's Daughters invited my Lady as came down and gave a Glass of good wine.

"As I came down again through the Gate I ask'd my Lady's Leave that now I might call it Bellomont Gate.

[150]

My Lady laugh'd and said, What a Complement he puts on me! With pleasancy."

Royal governors brought royal ships and royal troops, and redcoats and gold lace became a common sight on streets, in taverns, and even in the Congregational churches, though King's Chapel provided a service according to the Established Church.

In 1693 a fleet from the West Indies brought the yellow fever to Boston and Cotton Mather was very nearly exposed to it. For all the deadly infection, he set out one Sunday morning down the harbor to pray and preach " among an *herd,* that were so infectious, in probability it would have cost mee my Life," but he was taken " vehemently sick " on board the " Governour's Barge, in the Harbour," and his friends made him return home. He recovered once he touched dry land, and in the afternoon preached in his own church " where the *Admiral,* and principal Commanders of the Fleet came to hear mee. Knowing the horrid *Atheism,* and *Wickedness* of these that were now come to bee my Hearers, I preached unto them, on Psal. 119. 59, and my God help'd me in it. I believe, 'twas a *Good Angel,* which there struck mee *sick;* and by the Ministrations of those good and kind Spirits, I beleeve, I was afterwards, putt upon such Methods as God blessed for the Preservacōn of my Health."

The natural result of the new interests and varied life of Boston was to develop birth and position to self-consciousness, which strengthened as Boston men descended farther and farther from their ancestors. But the constant intermarriage of Boston families begot a wider and wider divergence from the families in the country. Four generations of life in New England had developed a rural class who looked with awe upon the townspeople to whom they owed money and upon whom they were dependent for marketing their produce.

Sarah Kemble Knight, a Boston lady of elegant accomplishments, who could write easy verse and who had a pretty satirical wit, on her journey to New York in 1704 was struck by nothing more than by the clownishness of the country bumpkins whom she met on her travels. A rude lot they were, with none of the dignity of the settlers of the heroic age. Only a few miles from Boston she found herself in a wilderness. " When we had Ridd about an how'r, wee came into a thick swamp, wch. by Reason of a great fogg, very much startled mee, it being now very Dark. . . .

" In about an how'r, or something more, after we left the Swamp, we come to Bilinges where I was to Lodg. My Guide dismounted and shew'd the door, signing to me wth his hand to Go in; wch I Gladly did — But had not gone many steps into the Room ere I was Interogated by a young Lady I understood afterwards was the Eldest daughter of the family, with these, or words to this purpose, (viz.) Law for mee — what in the world brings You here at this time a night? — I never see a woman on the Rode so Dreadfull late, in all the days of my versall life. Who are You? Where are You going? I'me scar'd out of my witts — with much more of the same Kind. I stood aghast, Prepareing to reply, when in comes my Guide — to him Madam turn'd, Roreing out: Lawfull heart, John, is it You? — how de do! Where in the world are you going with this woman? Who is she? John made no Ansr. but sat down in the corner, fumbled out his black Junk, and saluted that instead of Debb; she then turned agen to mee and fell anew into her silly questions, without asking me to sitt down. . . . I paid honest John wth money and dram according to contract, and Dismist him, and pray'd Miss to shew me where I must Lodg. Shee conducted me to a parlour in a little back Lento, wch was almost fill'd wth the bedsted, wch was so high that I was forced to climb on a chair to gitt up to ye wretched bed that lay on it; on wch having Strecht my tired Limbs, and lay'd my head on a Sad-coloured pillow, I began to think on the transactions of ye past day."

v

But though he might visit and pray with these rude country folk when they fell afoul of the law, they did not make part of Cotton Mather's congregation, who, as he himself said, were mostly of the middle way of life, neither poor nor rich. The social climbers followed Lord Bellomont to the services of the Established Church, or the colony's rich men to the Brattle Street Church. To these Cotton Mather could preach on Lecture Day and with them he often dined; with the very poor he came into contact constantly by his own efforts to do good. His charity list was always large, often including ninety pensioners. When the Biblical tenth of his income devoted to charity was used up, he would dip the deeper in his pocket; when all was gone he would pray; and then his prayers would find answer when a wealthy parishioner would put in his hands a truly large sum to be dispensed for charity. And to such as were beyond material help, to prisoners of all sorts, he administered spiritual help. In this way he came in contact with sordid murderers and romantic pirates.

In these years and for many years later pirates preyed upon English commerce. The line between privateering and piracy was purely imaginary; and privateering brought to colonial ports profits which were very inviting. Governor Bellomont was glad to escape unscathed from the scandal in which Captain Kidd's exploits involved not only him, but noble lords in England and even the king. Kidd was imprisoned in Boston in July, 1699. In April of that year Cotton Mather " visited the Prison. A great Number of Pyrates being there committed, besides other Malefactors, I went and pray'd with them, and preach'd to them. The Text, in which the Lord helped mee to Discourse, was Jer. 2. 26. *The Thief is ashamed, when hee is found.* I hope, I shall have some Fruit of these Endeavours." In the next January he preached again to " Pyrates on Jer. 17. 11. *Hee getts Riches and not by right; leaves them in the midst of his Dayes, and in his End shal be a Fool."* Pirates continued to harry the New England coast, however, and near the close of his life Cotton Mather had the privilege of preaching a sermon " At the Desire, and In the Hearing, of two Pyrates that are to dy Two Days hence. To a great Assembly, and with a great Assistence." To him these last services were a call to ministerial labors, but to the Boston populace they

were a public show. And just as today a condemned criminal is permitted to choose his last gustatory treat, so those
of the seventeenth century were permitted to choose the
minister for their last spiritual treat.

Another kind of pirates, the Moors on the Barbary
coast, were much less romantic and much more distressing. Many a poor sailor ended his days in Moorish captivity. New Englanders were interested in these poor
slaves, though they could do little except wish them well.
In 1698 Sewall sent to a friend abroad thanks for " the
frequent Notices . . . as to the poor Captives in Algeer
or Sally. I have inclosed 2 or 3 of M^r. Cotton Mathers
Pastoral Letters which He has written to direct and comfort them. As I formerly wrote to you, you had best remit
some of the Money in your hands to them for Support.
Thereby tis hoped the Bitterness of their Bondage may
be mitigated."

VI

With all the interests of these years Cotton Mather
still found time for the absorbing duties of an important
church, duties which he was ever extending into larger
fields until he was himself carrying on in some measure
activities for which the modern church requires a staff
of trained assistants. In his utter seriousness of purpose
he directed not only his days but his tongue: " May I
studiously decline to utter any thing, that I may foresee,
will be *useless,* much more, every thing that may be *hurt-
ful,* and *sinful,* to bee uttered. It must bee my Ambition,
every where to speak *usefully* and only those things, that
some one may bee the *better* or the *wiser* for." This pur-

pose he carried further in regard to his children, for he believed that he ought never to let them come into his presence nor ought he ever pass them by even when they were at play, or especially when they were at play, without letting fall some remark that would be at once interesting and useful and if possible memorable. With such intentions for the least words of his mouth it is small wonder that he found the days too short for him. Again and again in the course of his life he lamented his slothful habits and determined to get up earlier in the morning — his rising hour was never before eight. But like many a frailer mortal he found bed more enticing than good resolutions, and there is no record of his rising to greet the sun.

Besides his preaching — sometimes as often as five times in a single week — he was active in " praying and pious Meetings " in his neighbourhood. And he helped organize various societies. The Society for the Propagation of the Christian Religion fared well enough, but for the Society for the Suppression of Disorders there were inconveniently many applicants. This society was " composed of from each of our three Churches. But their Number is too large, to admitt any more: And yett there is a considerable Number that would gladly engage in the same noble Design with them. Wherefore I erected two more such *Societies;* one for the *North* End of the Town; one for the *South*." Even at this time the godly were humanly curious. And Cotton Mather's later proposal to list " the wicked Houses in the Town " shows that they had sufficient material to work upon.

[156]

Another society which came to Cotton Mather for help was a company of negroes " to meet the *Evening* after the *Sabbath* " to sing a psalm, to pray twice, and to hear a sermon. The negroes were not to come without leave of their maſters; they were not to use the meetings as an excuse to go elsewhere; they were to avoid wicked company, " the Sin of *Drunkenness,* or *Swearing,* or *Cursing* or *Lying,* or *Stealing,* or notorious *Disobedience* or *Unfaithfulness* to their Maſters." And " If any of our Society defile himself with *Fornication,* wee will give him our *Admonition;* and so debar him from the Meeting, at leaſt *half a Year.* . . ." Moreover, the members of the Society bound themselves not to run away from their maſters, to give no shelter to runaways, and to do their beſt to capture and punish those who ran away. There is no record that slaveholders gave Cotton Mather a vote of thanks.

He could thus guide slaves in the path of righteousness because he knew their shortcomings and ungratefulness from experience. His own slave, Onesimus, purchased for him as a gift from some of his parishioners, " at the expence of between forty and fifty Pounds," in spite of ten years' residence with his pious maſter who tried to oversee his education that he might read, " go on to Writing . . . be frequently Catechised," and spend his " liesure-hours " advantageously, proved " wicked . . . , useless, Froward, Immorigerous. My Disposing of him, and my Supplying my Family with a better Servant in his Room, requires much Caution, much Prayer, much Humiliation before the Lord. Repenting of what may have offended Him, in the case of my Servants, I would wait on Him, for his Mercy." In 1700 Samuel Sewall had published an anti-slavery tract, *The Selling of Joseph,* for which he received but " Frowns and hard Words "; nevertheless the earnest judge, believing it to be the " brest-work " of a necessary campaign, reprinted the pamphlet six years later when he " saw a very severe Act passing against Indians & Negroes." This was a " Bill against fornication, or Marriage of White men with Negros or Indians; with extraordinary penalties. . . . If it be pass'd, I fear twill be an Opression provoking to God, and that which will promote Murders and other Abominations." Sewall was fortunately in a position of sufficient power and influence to get " the Indians out of the Bill, and some mitigation for [the Negroes] left in it, and the clause about their Masters not denying their Marriage." This mitigating clause sponsored by Sewall read: " And no master shall unreasonably deny marriage to his negro with one of the same nation, any law, usage, or custom to the contrary notwithstanding." In a time when negro babies were of so little account that they were sometimes given away like a litter of puppies, slaves were expected to conform to a chaste continence not required of or practiced by their masters.

Cotton Mather's solution of the injustice (which he did not admit) of slavery was the conversion of the slaves to an active Christianity. Sewall, however, felt that " *Forasmuch as* Liberty *is in real value next unto* Life: *None ought to part with it themselves, or deprive others of it, but upon the most mature Consideration.*"

[158]

Cotton Mather, feeling as the mass of his contemporaries did, that slavery was divinely ordained, nevertheless permitted his Onesimus to take his thievish tendencies elsewhere, by purchase of his freedom. " My servant *Onesimus,* having advanced a Summ, towards the purchase of a Negro-Lad, who may serve many occasions of my Family in his Room, I do by this Inſtrument, Release him so far from my Service and from the claims that any under or after me might make unto him, that he may Enjoy and Employ his whole Time for his own purposes, and as he pleases. But upon these conditions. Firſt, that he do every Evening visit my Family, and prepare and bring in, the Fuel for the day following, so Long as the Incapacity of my present Servant, shall oblige us to Judge it necessary: As also, in great snows, appear seasonably with the help of the Shovel, as there shall be occasion.

" Secondly, that when the Family shall have any Domeſtic Business more than the Daily affairs, he shall be ready, upon being told of it so far to lend an helping Hand, as will give no Large nor Long Interruption to the Business, of his own, to which I have dismissed him; As particularly, to carry corn unto the mill, and help in the fetching of water for the washing, if we happen to be deſtitute. And in the piling of our wood, at the season of its coming in.

" Whereas also, the said *Onesimus* has gott the money which he has advanced as above mention'd, from the Liberties he took, while in my Service, and for some other Considerations, I do expeɕt, that he do within six months pay me the sum of Five Pounds, wherein he acknowledged himself Endebted to me."

Onesimus obviously had not been ill-treated. He had apparently been given much freedom; and when he "newly buried his Son; (*Onesimus* his *Onesimulus*)" his master twice took occasion to pray for and with him.

Indeed, Mather felt it his duty always to be of service to those in trouble of any kind. And he was constantly under the necessity by vote of the church, of censuring, admonishing, or excommunicating offenders. Adultery; bearing a child before the legal time after marriage; "consulting an ungodly Fortune-Teller"; "Revelling and Drunkenness"; stealing and lying; "a very indiscreet Action" of Abiel Loresen "in going and lodging aboard a Frigate"; Edward Mills' "taking a scandalous Liberty at the *Games* which the Law hath declared unlawfull" when he was under censure for sharing in the guilt of a "horrible Adulteress"; Abigail Day's "Expressions full of scandalous Discontent and Impatience under her Afflictions. Especially, saying of laudable Diet in the Almshouse, where she is lodged, that she would thank neither God nor Man for such Victuals" — these and many other entries in Cotton Mather's manuscript records of his church, show a church eager to keep itself uncontaminated.

The population of the town kept busy all ministers with a desire to reform them. The "Love of Rum [was] beyond all Imagination"; and "The woful Decay of good *Family-Discipline,* hath opened the Flood-gates, for Evils, innumerable, and almost irremediable." Cotton

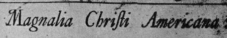

Magnalia Christi Americana:

OR, THE

Ecclesiastical History

OF

NEW-ENGLAND,

FROM

Its First Planting in the Year 1620. unto the Year
of our LORD, 1698.

In Seven BOOKS.

I. Antiquities: In Seven Chapters. With an Appendix.

II. Containing the Lives of the Governours, and Names of the Magistrates of *New-England:* In Thirteen Chapters. With an Appendix.

III. The Lives of Sixty Famous Divines, by whose Ministry the Churches of *New-England* have been Planted and Continued.

IV. An Account of the University of *Cambridge* in *New-England;* in Two Parts. The First contains the Laws, the Benefactors, and Vicissitudes of *Harvard College;* with Remarks upon it. The Second Part contains the Lives of some Eminent Persons Educated in it.

V. Acts and Monuments of the Faith and Order in the Churches of *New-England,* passed in their Synods; with Historical Remarks upon those Venerable Assemblies; and a great Variety of Church-Cases occurring, and resolved by the Synods of those Churches: In Four Parts.

VI. A Faithful Record of many Illustrious, Wonderful Providences, both of Mercies and Judgments, on divers Persons in *New-England:* In Eight Chapters.

VII. *The Wars of the Lord.* Being an History of the Manifold Afflictions and Disturbances of the Churches in *New-England,* from their Various Adversaries, and the Wonderful Methods and Mercies of God in their Deliverance: In Six Chapters: To which is subjoined, An Appendix of Remarkable Occurrences which *New-England* had in the Wars with the *Indian Salvages,* from the Year 1688, to the Year 1698.

By the Reverend and Learned *COTTON MATHER, M. A.*
And Pastor of the North Church in *Boston, New-England,*

LONDON:

Printed for *Thomas Parkhurst,* at the *Bible* and *Three*
Crowns in *Cheapside.* MDCCII.

TITLE PAGE OF THE *Magnalia,* LONDON, 1702

Mather felt impelled to make a list of the reprehensible things in Massachusetts, from the " *Vanity of Apparel* . . . affected by many persons, who have been so *vain,* as to *glory in their Shame* " — and yet the learned doctor himself wore a periwig; to the " hellish *Cursing, Wicked Sorceries,* [and] the Sins of *Uncleanness* in many and the grossest Instances." Preaching, as he did, repeated sermons for condemned criminals, he saw much of life's sordidness. When he preached for Sarah Threeneedles, " condemned to dy, for murdering her base-born Child," the streets were filled with the overflow from the church.

Cotton Mather prayed and preached for sinners of high life and low life; he prayed with apparently equal fervour for domestic comforts and for the downfall of Empires. In 1696 in a day of secret fast he mingled appeals; asking for " Mercy for this Land in its deplorable Circumstances, and a mighty Revolution upon the Kingdomes of Great *Britain* and upon the French Empire. As well as to obtain the special Assistences of Grace for the various Concerns of my Ministry; and the safety of my many particular Friends now going to sea, and my affayrs with them."

He was fully conscious of the burden of his pastorate, for he wrote, " among the *Protestants,* the very same *individual Man,* must preach, catechise, administer the Sacraments, visit the afflicted, and manage all the parts of Church-Discipline; and if any *Books,* for the service of Religion bee written, Persons thus *extremely encumbered* must bee the *Writers.* Now, of all the Churches under Heaven, there are none that expect so much Varietie of

[161]

Service from their Paſtors, as those of *New England;* and of all the Churches in *New England,* there are none that require more, than those in *Boſton,* the *Metropolis* of the English *America.* . . . Conſtant *Sermons,* usually more than once, and perhaps three or four Times in a Week, and all the other Duties of a *paſtoral Watchfulness,* a very *large Flock* hath all this while demanded of mee; nor hath my Station left me free from Obligations to spend very much Time, in the *evangelical Service* of *others* also."

VII

In spite of this ſtaggering aĉtivity Cotton Mather made a ſtart upon what he regarded as his literary life-work, to which his mountainous bibliography was merely incidental: " an huge number of *golden Keyes,* to open the *Pandeĉts* of Heaven, and some Thousands of charming and singular Notes, by the *new Help* whereof, the *Word of CHRIST may run and bee glorified.* If the *God of my Life,* will please to spare my Life . . . I may make unto the Church of God, an humble Tender of our BIBLIA AMERICANA, a Volumn *enriched* with better Things, than all the *Plate* of the *Indies*; yett not I, but the Grace of Chriſt with mee." Though he worked upon this gigantic undertaking all the reſt of his life, it was never published.

He was more fortunate with what is regarded as his title to a place in American literature, his *Magnalia Chriſti Americana* or *The Ecclesiaſtical Hiſtory of New-England,* printed in England in 1702 as a folio of 788 pages. Cotton Mather had sent it to London in 1700 and had prayed regularly and eagerly for its success. He had

had " great Perswasions and Assurances of His Blessing "
upon it; he had feared its loss and humiliated himself before God for it; and at laſt in October, 1702, he firſt saw
it. " Wherefore, I sett apart this Day, for solemn THANKS-
GIVING unto God, for His watchful and gracious Providence over that Work, and for the Harveſt of so many
Prayers, and Cares, and Tears, and Resignations, as I had
employ'd upon it."

He had indeed produced a book invaluable for the
modern ſtudent of American hiſtory. He had set out to
show how great had been the men of the heroic age of the
settlement of Massachusetts, to what trials they had been
subjećted, what difficulties they had overcome, with what
zeal they had organized their lives and their churches for
the greater glory of their God, and what remarkable
evidences of the Divine interposition in their affairs the
hiſtory of the colony showed. It contains biographies,
hiſtorical summaries, sermons, and theological exposi-
tions. It is written from the thoroughly biased point of
view of one who saw nothing in the seventy years of Massachusetts that needed defence, who was sublimely unaware that there was another side than he presented. The
ſtyle is the beſt of a kind which now appears completely
vicious. The book is crowded with " conceits," ornament,
Latin quotations, periphrases, and turgid dićtion. But for
what it set out to be it is superb. No single work throws
more light upon the miniſters and magiſtrates of the seventeenth-century Massachusetts Commonwealth and their
point of view.

It is clear from the *Magnalia* that the ruling caſte of

Massachusetts sincerely believed that in establishing the colony they were working for God. He had put upon them the Christian's burden of governing a large majority of very frail souls rendered the more prone to sin by the roughness, privation, monotony, drudgery, and danger of pioneer life; by the presence at their doors of a wild subject race, moody and resentful, which might at any time burst into murderous fury; by the gathering of dissolute and reckless seafarers, adventurers, and traders; and by the emergence from time to time, within the ranks of the faithful, of capable and intelligent heretics whose ideas, were they to receive general acceptance, would completely undermine the authority of the rulers and surrender territory held in trust for God to the control of the very real and very powerful Satan from whom they had wrested it.

In such an atmosphere there could be no toleration for religious dissent. The rulers of Massachusetts had no doubt of their possession of the truth about God. The men of Marblehead might cry out that their main end in coming to the New World was to catch fish, but the men of Marblehead were an unregenerate lot whom the angels had abandoned as a bad job.

The Massachusetts men who were on the side of the angels showed no more mercy to themselves than they showed to the Quakers and the Antinomians, whom they ruthlessly banished and who appear in the *Magnalia* in their blackest garments. The Christianity which Cotton Mather outlined in this book was no easy faith. Before it yawned the hideous doom of those who were condemned to everlasting flame. The core of this religion was the firmly rooted belief in original sin. The Puritans of Massachusetts were brutally frank, not only in their language, but also in the assumption that every man in his natural state, that is, before he had been converted to the brand of Protestantism fathered by Calvin, was a sink of iniquity.

They had no reluctance in exposing to light and air the vices which now are regarded as too hideous even to be mentioned. There was then no suspicion of morbidity attaching to the man who showed a special interest in ingenious and darkly interesting sins. Ministers had no hesitation then in fully exploiting in their sermons the rich and variegated English vocabulary of evil. The prudishness which is now called Puritan was utterly un-characteristic of the men of Puritan Boston. They burned with zeal to root out every form of evil, but they had not the least desire to root out of books, sermons, conversation, or their thoughts the description of evil. Indeed, men repressed as they were found an excellent outlet in speech. The congregation which listened to a godly and reverend minister preaching as Thomas Shepard preached must have breathed more freely at the end:

" Every natural man and woman is born full of all sin, as full as a toad is of poison, as full as ever his skin can hold; mind, will, eyes, mouth, every limb of his body, and every piece of his soul, is full of sin . . . thy mind is a nest of all the foul opinions, heresies, that ever were vented by any man; thy heart is a foul sink of all atheism, sodomy, blasphemy, murder, whoredom, adultery, witchcraft, buggery; so that, if thou haſt any good thing in thee, it is but as a drop of rose-water in a bowl of poison; where fallen it is all corrupted."

Perhaps the high value which Chriſtianity has always set upon repentance had something to do with the seventeenth-century preoccupation with sinners. If "joy shall be in heaven over one sinner that repenteth, more than over ninety and nine juſt persons, which need no repentance," there was plenty of reason for ſtressing crime. And the seventeenth century knew plenty of crime. Moreover, since religious fervour and abnormal sexuality are divided by only the thinneſt line, one might suspeſt that it was the violations of the seventh commandment that were dwelt upon with greateſt zeal. Pioneer life was hard and meager, especially in the frontier villages; organized amusements were almoſt wholly lacking; and continual brooding upon evil brought the inevitable result. Everywhere in the *Magnalia* one finds burſting through the conventional layer of piety and conformity evidences of morbidity and criminality. From the beginning there had come to Massachusetts numbers of men and women who broke down under the ſtrain of frontier life. Servants, mechanics, laborers, and slaves formed a proletariat even in early Boſton; and the gallows, the whipping poſt, the ſtocks, and the pillory were kept busy. However savage the penalties, it is clear from the *Magnalia* that crime flourished. Cotton Mather was particularly intereſted in adultery, murder, and rape, and colleſted many examples of confessions on the gallows and of execution sermons. In moſt cases punishment was ac-

[166]

companied by remarkable manifestations which could be interpreted only as evidences of the divine will. Mary Martin, for instance, in 1646 had killed her newborn child. She confessed and was sentenced to death. " That renown'd man, old Mr. Cotton . . . preached a sermon on Ezek. xvi 20, 21; ' Is this of thy whoredom a small matter, that thou hast slain my children? ' . . . But there was this remarkable at her execution: she acknowledged her *twice* essaying to kill her child before she could make an end of it: and now, through the unskillfulness of the executioner, she was turned off the ladder twice before she died."

Particularly revolting according to modern ideas were the frequent cases of " bestiality," or sexual relations of men and animals, a crime explained in detail as late as 1803 in connection with the discussion of the seventh commandment in *An Explanation of the Shorter Catechism.* Though punishable by death, this crime in the seventeenth century flourished more widely than the extent of the population seems to warrant. When it occurred it was made no secret. People knew about it, discussed it, made solemn warning of it, and attended the grotesque executions of these " diabolical " men along with sundry cows, heifers, sheep, and pigs, their companions in the crime.

There was one especially extraordinary occurrence: " At the southward there was a beast, which brought forth a creature which might pretend to something of an human shape. Now, the people minded that the *monster* had a blemish in one eye, much like what a profligate

[167]

fellow in the town was known to have. This fellow was hereupon examined; and upon his examination, confess'd his infandous Beſtialities; for which he was deservedly executed."

Whether these cases of morbid crime were true or false is not important; what is important is that they were told freely, read freely, and freely believed; that they come not from hearsay or from some obscure or "curious" source, but from the *Magnalia* of Cotton Mather, a book written to glorify Puritans and to defend Puritanism. When one realizes the complete lack of prudishness or even common reticence among Puritan men and women, the prevalent modern conception of the "Puritanical" seems grotesque.

VIII

At the close or beginning of each year Cotton Mather was wont to liſt his mercies. The year then began with the 1ſt of March, so that September was indeed truly the seventh and December the tenth month. In April, early in the year 1700, Cotton Mather held a day of secret thanksgiving for his liſt of more than a pageful of mercies. In the light of what followed in this year of troubles it holds a pathetic irony, for here among subſtantial blessings such as his "extraordinary *Library,* and the Possession of several thousands of books," his "grown and . . . great *Salary,* and . . . comfortable Habitation," he liſts his "desireable *Consort*" and his "*Reputation,* preserved from ill Men, and embalmed with good Men."

It was in this year that there began for him a series of domeſtic troubles sufficient to crush the spirit of one less patient, humble, and devout. Mather was destined to lose two wives; and the deaths of both wives, a decade apart, were accompanied with the serious illness and death of children. Misfortunes beset him on every hand; with the Brattle Street Church to bother him, his father's difficulties with Harvard to plague him, and with the political field bristling with thorns, his " *Faith* was now tried. . . . Wonderful the Trial of my *Faith*. But it held out comfortably under the Trial." Had Mather grown bitter and resentful under all this oppression from without and within, he could not have been accounted remiss. But with a faith that really relied upon God, he found in prayer a satisfaction of all his doubts, of all his pains. And in what he thought was direct assurance that God would hear him, watch over him and his, and console him amply for all his griefs, he found an exalting consolation.

In October, 1700, Mrs. Mather's health became a matter of great concern. She suffered from " sore throat and such Tumour and such Dolour and such Danger of Choaking, and such Exhausting of her Strength with it, as is not common." Poor young woman! Married before she was sixteen, at thirty she had had fourteen years of child-bearing and child-tending. Now in December she bore a son over whom his father could raise no " *Particular Faith* " of the Lord's acceptance of the child. So sure was he that it would " dy in its Infancy " that he took " the Liberty to express " this doubt to his father and to his weak wife. His feeling was soon justified, for this Samuel, after outliving " more than an hundred very

[169]

terrible Fitts," died less than two months after birth. Sixteen months later Mrs. Mather had a miscarriage, and with this her career of motherhood ended with but four of her many children alive. For months she lingered, raised from her bed occasionally by her husband's earnest prayers. While she lay ill three of her children, besides a maidservant, contracted smallpox, and their learned father gave up his study to them for a hospital. In all his worry over wife and children he yet lamented the necessity of yielding up this stronghold of privacy. He prayed with his children at their request " ten or a dozen times a day "; and yet found time to pray for and with his neighbours, many of whom were ill with smallpox. He comforted his wife " with as lively Discourses upon the Glory of Heaven, whereto she was going as I could make unto her. I disposed her, and myself, all that I could, unto a glorious Resignation," he pathetically writes in his diary. By this time Mrs. Mather was so worn out with suffering — she seems to have had cancer of the breast — that she needed little to make her resigned. Her husband had, indeed, frequently in prayer been assured by the Lord that she would recover; but after a while, though he continued his fasts and prayers for her life, he began to feel that perhaps the Lord was merely delaying her death until she and her husband were the " better prae-pared for it." All possible remedies were tried, even those which came to her in dreams where a " grave Person " advised her for the " intolerable pain in her Breast " to apply warm wool cut from a living sheep. And " for her Salivation, which hitherto nothing had releeved, said

[170]

he, take a Tankard of Spring-Water, and therein over the Fire dissolve an agreeable Quantity of Maſtic's, and of Gum Isinglass: drink of this Liquor now and then, to ſtrengthen the Glands, which ought to have been done a great while ago." But this, beyond relieving the fever a little, proved of no avail. She died, having lived with her husband " juſt as many Years as she had lived in the World, before she came to me; with an Addition of the seven Months, wherein her dying Languishments were preparing me to part with her. When I had been married unto her juſt sixteen Years, (and as near as I can recollect, on that very Week, sixteen Years, that I was married unto her) God began to take her from me." Two hours before she died he took into his " a dear Hand, the deareſt in the World," and then solemnly and sincerely resigning her to the Lord, he " putt her gently out of " his hands resolving never to touch her any more. This, he felt, was " the hardeſt and perhaps the braveſt Action " of his life. Mrs. Mather who had before conſtantly called for him now recognized their parting as final. Her relief was at hand. Cotton Mather himself preached the funeral sermon, ſtudying that the sorrow of his " Family, might prove an occasion of Goodness on others." He was deeply touched by the sympathy of his congregation and its expression in the building of " a coſtly Tomb, for the Ashes of my lovely Consort, and of my Children, whereof there were five buried, with no more than common *grave* Stones."

The three victims of smallpox recovered, as did also the maid, who, however, became so diſtracted as to be dismissed, to return later, recovered, as a special answer to Mather's prayer for a good servant.

Now Cotton Mather feeling that all muſt be for the beſt in a divinely ordained world, set himself to juſtify God's aǎion in taking away his " lovely," his " desireable consort." Her months of excessive pain, her extended career of nine babies and we know not how many miscarriages, he did not think it necessary to consider or to juſtify. But he did see that in designing her death God had dealt kindly with her, though her husband's " extravagant Fondness for her, would upon any Terms have detained her here." A few days before she died she had expressed the fear that she would make her attendants weary with her long invalidism, though she excepted her husband: *" I don't mean you,* Mr. Mather! " " Nevertheless," records her grieving husband, " my Health would infallibly have been deſtroy'd, if she had recovered a little more, and so far that I should have run the venture of sleeping with her. My feeble Conſtitution, would undoubtedly have run into a Consumption. And my Children would also have suffered miserably in their Education. But more than all this; she was a Gentlewoman of a melancholy Temper; and there were some dreadful Changes on her Father's Family. He had extremely broken her Spirit, by bringing home a Mother-in-law, tho' he did well in it. Her youngeſt Brother, and a considerable Intereſt of mine with him, (some hundreds of Pounds perhaps) was newly fallen into the Hands of the French Enemy. Her second Brother, who was her Darling, I had almoſt said, her Idol, was dead in *London,* whither he went the laſt Winter. Her eldeſt Brother proves an idle, profane, drunken, and sottish Fellow, and a Disgrace to all his Relatives, and haſtens apace to Ruine. . . . The sight of these Things, would have brought such a Disorder of Mind upon her, as would have rendred my Condition insupportable." She had indeed said, — and " with a more than ordinary Passion and Agony " — when her favorite brother went to London, *" that she desired, God would never lett her live to hear of the Death of that* young man! " Though her family knew of his death, it was kept from her because of her feeble ſtate of health; and by a ſtrange coincidence the letter written to her by his landlady arrived three hours after this highſtrung young woman had gone to her reſt.

The day after her funeral her husband held a day of secret faſt, prayer, and humiliation to obtain pardon for all the sins for which the Lord was now chaſtising him. There seems to have been no doubt in his mind that misfortune was ever the price of sin; hence the arrival of misfortune meant soul-searching for the sin. At the beginning of his wife's fatal illness she had " unhappily miscarried of a son . . . and yett, it is possible, that not unhappily; for she had also a *false Conception,* whereof she was now delivered. . . .

" I thought it my Duty to humble myself before the Lord, under His Rebukes upon my Family. And I could find sufficient Occasions for Humiliation. But when I more particularly examined, Whether I had ever troubled the Churches of the Lord, with any *false Conception,* I could not find myself Conscious to any such Matter."

[173]

The month following his wife's death he devoted one day a week to fasting and prayer, feeling that it was " now Time . . . to look back a little, on the Dispensations of Heaven, that have been rolling over me. Has not the Death of my Consort, that most astonishing Sting in it; *a Miscarriage of a Particular Faith!* Truly, nothing has ever yett befallen me, that has come so near to it."

And when the next month his " pretty little Nanny " came near death with a violent fever attended by agonizing convulsions, he was ready to resign himself to the loss of this favorite child. But though she was aware that her father had " given [her] away," this baby, not yet five years old, declared that she would *" not dy this Time, for all that! "* The Lord intervened in her behalf as her father prayed for her, and " A most watchful Providence of Heaven saved the Child from taking a Paper of powdered *Cantharides* [a dangerous aphrodisiac] which by a Mistake between the Doctor, and one of my Servants, had been given to the Child, instead of a paper of *Ens Veneris."*

When to the astonishment of all this daughter, who in spite of frequent sickness outlived her father, recovered, Cotton Mather recorded one of the few bits of philosophy to be found in his voluminous diary: " I must not forgett my fervent and zelous Desire, that whatever *Calamity* befals me in this present evil World, my Lord JESUS CHRIST may have Revenues of Glory and Service out of it. I have been most signally gratified in this Desire, and a *Calamity* in some sort ceases to be one, when I am so."

That his griefs might count for the glory of the Lord by edifying others, he prepared for publication the funeral sermons he had preached for his wife and children, prefacing them with a prayer: " *O Father of Mercies;* What shall I render to thee for thy wonderful Mercies to me, the *Chief of Sinners!* Will the Lord indeed make use of sinful me, and not only of my *Labours,* but of my *Sorrowes* also, to do some little Good among his chosen People . . . ! If the Lord will break me, and *my House* to peeces, but make it an Occasion to build *His House; . . .* what an aſtonishing *Alleviation* does this give to all my *Afflictions.* Lord, in *Faithfulness Thou haſt afflicted me.* Bless the Lord, O my Soul, for all His Benefits! "

And the weekly faſt days continued that in the cultivation of his soul he might conquer the fleshly temptations which now beset him. Though he daily and literally prostrated himself before the Lord, he was not happy. Up to this time he had " rarely known any Tears, except those that were for the Joy of the Salvation of God. But now, scarce a Day passes me without a Flood of Tears, and my Eyes even Decay with weeping."

He had not long before this lamented, " If I had not a very *earthly Heart,* how much might I live in *Heaven,* while on *Earth!* " But though he often addressed Heaven with prayers " no less than ten several Times " " between one a Clock and seven," he could not divorce himself from temporal affairs.

CHAPTER SIX

"I find a *Sacrificing Life* to be fuller of strong and
strange Consolations, than can be imagined
by one, who has made no Trial of it."

— *Diary of Cotton Mather*

I

IN all the bitterness of his father's defeat, one political
hope remained to Cotton Mather. In 1701 Lord Bellomont, who had succeeded Phips as governor, and
Stoughton, the lieutenant governor, both died. In their
place was appointed Joseph Dudley, who had had earlier
relations with the Mathers. In the months that passed
before Sir Edmund Andros had arrived in New England
Dudley was president of the Council; under Andros he
had held high office; and as a native of Massachusetts and
a graduate of Harvard he was, because of his relations
with Andros, hated as a turncoat and an oppressor of his
own people. During the revolution of 1689 he was imprisoned. He wrote piteous letters to Cotton Mather,
whose great influence at this time, when he still lacked
four years of being thirty, Dudley recognized. Mather
apparently helped to lighten his imprisonment. He continued to beg for help even in such details as that he had
been " allowed no victuals till nine of the clock at night,
when the keeper's wife offered to kindle her own fire
to warm something for me, and the corporal expresly
commanded the fire to be put out. — I may be easily

[176]

oppressed to death." In 1690 he had with Andros embarked for England. He returned to the colonies to serve the king as chief justice in New York, but after a few years went back to England, becoming a personage of importance as the lieutenant governor of the Isle of Wight and a member of Parliament. His chief ambition, however, was to return as royal governor to the province which had imprisoned and abused him. After the death of Bellomont he succeeded. His success was due to Cotton Mather, whose kindness had helped him in his dark days and whose letter assuring him that the ministers and members of the Assembly would welcome his coming he read to the King. Consequently, when in 1702 Dudley arrived, Cotton Mather might well believe that the future looked bright. Perhaps he saw himself, like his father, a maker of governors, a statesman-priest. But Joseph Dudley was no William Phips. He was a cunning, shrewd, relentless, high-handed politician; and though he was willing to use Cotton Mather for what he could get out of him, he knew well enough that the future lay with the Brattle Street-Harvard group.

Five days after Dudley had arrived as governor Cotton Mather wrote in his diary: " June 16. I received a Visit from Governour *Dudley*. Among other Things that I said to him, I used these words, ' Syr, you arrive to the Government of a People, that have their Various and their divided Apprehensions, about many things; and particularly about your own Government over them. I am humbly of Opinion, that it will be your wisdome, to carry an indifferent Hand towards all Parties; if in our case, I may use so Coarse a Word as Parties. And give Occasion unto none to say, that any have monopolized, you, or, that you take your measures from them alone. I will explain myself, with the Freedome, and the Justice, (perhaps, the Prudence,) that you may expect from me. I will do no otherwise than I would be done to. I should be content I would approve it, and commend it, if any one should say to your Excellency; *By no means lett any People have cause to say, that you take all your Measures from the two Mr. Mathers.* By the same Rule, I may say without offence; *by no means lett any People say, that you go by no Measures in your Conduct, but* Mr. Byfield's, *and* Mr. Leveret's. This I speak, not from any personal Prejudice against the Gentlemen, but from a due Consideration of the Disposition of the People; and as a Service to your Excellency.'

" The Wretch went unto those Men and told them, that I had advised him, to be no ways advised by them: and inflamed them into an implacable Rage against me." Cotton Mather was learning that he who plays with politics is like to burn his fingers.

Joseph Dudley was having his hands full with an Assembly dominated by his enemies, blocking him wherever possible, determined to yield ground to royal demands only an inch at a time, and watching with eager anticipation for any grievance whereby their friends in England could attack him. For ten years Dudley had a war on his hands. While England fought with France thousands of miles away, the French of Canada and their Indian allies raided the colonial frontiers. There were no great fights as in King Philip's war, but a regular harassing of unprotected villages on the frontier. Coming close to Cotton Mather was the famous raid on Deerfield when the Reverend John Williams and his family were carried off to Canada. Mrs. Williams, who was killed on the march, was Cotton Mather's cousin. Mr. Williams and most of his children were later redeemed, but his eight-year-old daughter Eunice, preferring the free life of the savages to that of a parsonage, refused to leave the Indians, having, like them, become converted to Catholicism. One good Bostonian had hopes of her, " may be as when Samson married a Philistine." However, she remained faithful to her new church and to the Indian whom she in due time married. With him she visited her relatives in Longmeadow, but with him she returned to his people.

In 1711 Cotton Mather remembers that he has " a poor Kinswoman, a Daughter of my cosen-german . . . who has been six or seven years a Captive, in the hands of the French Popish Indians. I am afraid, I have not considered the miserable condition of that Child, with such a frequency and fervency of Supplication, as I should have done; tho' I have not forgotten it." In the same year he remembers her again with the added reflection, " And I would make her condition an Argument in Discourses with my own children, for Thankfulness and Piety." So he sought not only alleviation of his kinswoman's lot, but also edification from the consideration of " The dark Dispensation of Providence, which detains my poor Kinswoman, in her Indian Captivity "; but Eunice Williams remained a happy Indian squaw until her death in 1786.

[179]

The events of these Indian raids were long remembered, passing early into school-book histories. In Cotton Mather's mind they became atrocities blacker than those of King Philip's war, and later he used them against Dudley, who, as governor, could most easily be blamed for what was really the last far-flung backwash of the tide of European wars.

Now and again the colonists undertook expeditions against Canadian strongholds, usually without success. Dudley had little support from England, and the New England colonies were not inclined to work together. New England saw no reason to make sacrifices of money, men, and shipping to fight for a cause which had importance only for the European balance of power. Moreover, there was money to be made in trading with the French. In 1706 Cotton Mather, delivering the Thursday lecture, made occasion to denounce this " unlawful Trade, with our French and Indian Enemies," though his own brother-in-law, brother of his dead wife, was involved. The General Assembly fined the traders, of whom this John Phillips was one, and " On that Occasion it was necessary " for Mather, though " as easily, and as modestly," as he could, to join with the other ministers in " faithful Testimony." The wrath of his father-in-law descended upon him. The old man was in " a very froward and evil Frame," and expressed himself " very enragedly and abusively," aided by his two wicked sons. There was nothing for Mather to do but to take this vexing matter to the Lord and pray both for his misguided relatives-in-law and " that my Children may not be damnified," left their grandfather's wrath toward their father lead him to deal unjustly with them, and " forgett His Promises to their dying Mother." Obviously the gentleman had worldly possessions to bequeath, however tainted.

Governor Dudley himself was never above suspicion of making money by such traffic. He had risen to power by the chicanery and wire-pulling which constituted politics at the courts of William and of Anne, and he saw no objection to the same sort of practice in the New World. He had his following and he played an excellent political game. And he had able opponents. Elisha Cooke, the enemy of the Mathers, hated Dudley, too. Samuel Sewall, who was related to Dudley by marriage, worked against him on the Council; and Cotton Mather, though there was no open break at first, merely waited his time to pay back the " wretch " for his betrayal of confidence. It is no wonder that the governor's son Paul, who was attorney-general, wrote to England: " The government and college are disposed of here in chimney corners and private meetings, as confidently as can be. . . . "

Being sprung from the country, Governor Dudley naturally despised it as crude, coarse, and uncouth. In December, 1705, he quarreled with two farmers on a snow-drifted highway. Their version of the affair shows that New England farmers were stiff-necked seventy years before Concord and Lexington: " I, John Winchester, being upon the road in the lane . . ., hereing Mr. William Dudley give out threatening words that he would stab Trowbridge his horse, and run Trowbridge himself through the body if he did not turn out of the way, I left my cart and came up and laid down my whip by Trowbridge his team. I asked Mr. Dudley why he was so rash; he replyed ' this dog wont turn out of the way for the Governour.' . . . I, turning about and seeing Trowbridge his horses twisting about, ran to stop them to prevent damage . . . the Governour followed me with his drawn sword. . . . he struck me on the head with his sword, giveing me there a bloody wound. . . . I catcht hold on his sword, and it broke. . . . I called to the standers by to take notice that what I did was in defence of my life. Then the Governor said ' you lie, you dog; you lie, you divell,' repeating the same words divers times. Then said I, ' such words dont become a christian '; his Exelency replyed ' a christian, you dog, a christian, you divell, I was a christian before you were born.' I told him twas very hard that we who were true subjects and had bene allways ready to serve him in anything, should be so run upon; then his Exelency took up my cart whip and struck me divers blows: then said I ' what flesh and blood will bear this: ' his Exelency said ' why dont you run away, you Dog, you Divell, why don't you run away.' . . .

" When we spake of tarrying no longer but of driveing along our teams, his Exelency said ' no, you shall goe to Goale, you Dogs; ' when twas askt what should become of our teams his Exelency said, ' let them sink into the bottom of the earth.' "

After a few years of Dudley's administration, the time

seemed ripe for a carefully planned conspiracy to oust him, a conspiracy in which Cotton Mather played an important part. There was presented to Queen Anne in September, 1701, by " inhabitants in your majesty's dominions in America or trading thereto " a petition urging that Dudley be removed as governor, charging him with having countenanced a private trade and correspondence with the enemy, with having furnished them with ammunition and provisions, and with having been guilty of what amounted to treason. At the same time there was published and circulated in London *A Memorial of the present Deplorable State of New-England, With the many Disadvantages it lyes under, by the Male-Administration of their present Governour, Joseph Dudley, Esq. And his Son Paul, &c.* There is every reason to believe that this pamphlet was written by Cotton Mather. It may be assumed, therefore, that he was aware of the plan to present a petition to the Queen, and that he had gathered the material for the pamphlet and had sent it to London so that the presenters of the petition might have good ammunition in their attack. The pamphlet accuses the governor of trading with the enemy, of refusing to take measures to put down the enemy, of withholding attack with a view to increasing the expenditures of the colonies, of being " very Screwing and Exacting upon the People," and of hushing up scandals. These charges are sustained by letters and affidavits. Then, assuming that these charges will be accepted as true, the pamphlet blames Dudley for the prolongation of the war and hence with " several Barbarities " which have been committed by the Indians, following all with " some Memorable Providences " in the true Mather manner. That " no *English Woman* was ever known to have any Violence offered unto her *Chastity* " by any of the Indians is held not to the credit of the " Bruitish Salvages," but to the " Wonderful Reſtraint from God " upon them. Similarly, only God is responsible for the faċt that so few captives were killed by the Indians. " 'Tis wonderful," says the pamphlet, " that when many of the Captives have been juſt going to be Sacrificed, some ſtrange Interposition of the Divine Providence has put a ſtop to the Execution, and prevented their being made a Sacrifice." Then follows a satisfaċtory liſt of atrocities.

What Cotton Mather sought to gain by his part in the conspiracy may be variously interpreted. One may suggeſt, however, that he knew Willard, the vice-president of Harvard, to be ill and feeble; and he felt, were he to have a share in Dudley's downfall, he would be acceptable to the popular party in the Assembly and would be made the new president.

But nothing happened according to plan. In the month in which the petition was presented to Queen Anne, Vice-President Willard died. In Oċtober the " Fellows of Harvard College meet, and chuse Mr. Leverett President: He had eight votes, Dr. Increase Mather three, Mr. Cotton Mather, one, and Mr. Brattle of Cambridge, one." So Cotton Mather's hopes were gone, and the careful planning againſt Dudley would be of no use even if it succeeded. But it did not succeed. The Queen denied the petition, the governor got a vote of confidence from the Council, Cotton Mather would neither deny nor own the authorship of the pamphlet, and the *Deplorable State* was answered in London by a pamphlet which made it appear ridiculous. Cotton Mather was completely beaten, and the man who had helped defeat his father now sat in his father's seat at Harvard; a man one year older than Cotton Mather, with whom he had been a student at Harvard.

Of the Mathers' next act one must judge as his charity dictates. Was it rage and disappointment which prompted Increase and Cotton Mather to send in January, 1703, letters to the governor repeating all the charges that gossip, rumor, or an embittered imagination could lay at his door; and to print in London in 1708 a rejoinder to the answer to the first pamphlet? Or was it the noble and self-denying act of ministers who would speak the truth as they saw it no matter what the course? The letter of Increase is harsh but calm and measured; Cotton's is bitterly vituperative. How bitterly Cotton felt may be seen by a single paragraph in the conclusion of the letter: " Scores of times have my most intimate friends heard me formerly say, that although in the time of your *government*, you have treated me with much *aversion* (and would affront a gentleman for nothing, but the crime of giving me a *visit;* and would throw affronts upon gentlemen, merely for being *inhabitants* in *that part* of the town where I have my habitation;) yet if the troubles you brought on yourself should procure your abdication and recess into a more private condition, and your present *parasites* forsake you, as you *may be sure they will,* I should think it my duty to do you all the good offices imaginable." There is every indication here of a first-rate persecution mania.

The inner circles of Boston were now in an uproar. On January 31st Mr. Pemberton of the South Church talked to Sewall " very warmly about Mr. Cotton Mather's Letter to the Govr, seem'd to resent it, and expect the Govr should animadvert upon him. . . . Said if he were as the Govr he would humble him though it cost him his head; Speaking with great vehemency just as I parted with him at his Gate." On February 5th " Mr. Colman [of the Manifesto Church in Brattle Square] preaches the Lecture in Mr. Wadsworth's Turn, from Gal. 5. 25. If we live in the Spirit, let we also Walk in the Spirit. Spake of Envy and Revenge as the Complexion and Condemnation of the Devil; Spake of other walking; it blôted our sermons, blôted our Prayers, blôted our Admonitions and Exhortations. It might justly put us upon asking our selves whether we did live in the Spirit, whether we were ever truly regenerated, or no. 'Tis reckoned he lash'd Dr. Mather and Mr. Cotton Mather . . . for what they have written, preach'd and pray'd about the present Contest with the Govr."

On the 3rd of February Governor Dudley wrote from Roxbury to " the Reverend Doctors Mather " a dignified, calm, and telling reply. Even if the charges were true, he says, " yet I cannot but think that your manner of treating me can be justified by no principles of reason, religion, nay of common civility. The very spirit and temper of your letters will, I doubt not, appear to all indifferent persons to be the farthest from the spirit which

[186]

is pure, peaceable, and gentle?" Why, he asks, have the Mathers been silent all these years? "Surely murder, robberies, and other such flaming immoralities were as reproveable then as now. . . . Why then have you permitted me to go on in these evils, without admonition, till you tell me I have ruined myself, family, and country? . . . The articles are so many contained in your letters, that it would be endless to labour your satisfaction by writing, which you must not further expect from me. . . .

"I desire you will keep your station, and let fifty or sixty good ministers, your equals in the province, have a share in the government of the college, and advise thereabouts as well as yourselves, and I hope all will be well. . . .

"I am an honest man, and have lived religiously these forty years to the satisfaction of the ministers in New England; and your wrath against me is cruel, and will not be justified . . . the college must be disposed against the opinion of all the ministers in New England, except yourselves, or the Governour torn in pieces. This is the view I have of your inclination."

In the next year Cotton Mather noted: "The other Ministers of the Neighbourhood, are this Day feasting with our wicked Governour; I have by my provoking Plainness and Freedom, in telling this Ahab of his wickedness, procured myself to be left out of his Invitation. I rejoiced in my Liberty from the Temptations, with which they were encumbred, while they were *eating of his Dainties* and durst not *reprove* him. And, considering

[187]

the Power and Malice of my Enemies, I thought it proper for me, to be this day *Fasting,* in Secret, before the Lord." The grapes were very sour indeed.

II

But these political vexations were not Cotton Mather's only troubles. On his fortieth birthday his spirit had " felt several Irradiations from Heaven " and he had thought " what a Blessed Thing is the Righteousness of my Lord Jesus Christ; that a Man who has been horribly sinning for forty Years together, may stand in that Righteousness before God, and be treated and loved, as if he had been all this while in the exactest Manner glorifying the Lord."

He needed all the heavenly irradiations he could get, for within two months of his wife's death he was " considering how frequently and foolishly Widowers miscarry." Troubled as he was with an insistent body, he prayed that rather than dishonor God, he be granted the immediate favor of death. He was startled with a more immediate answer than he had expected: " I found myself grow very ill; I thought myself arrested with an high Feavour; I suspected, that the Lord was going to take me at my own Word. But now, I perceived it was nothing but *Vapours.*"

More substantial was a " very astonishing Trial " which almost directly upon his wife's death appeared in the form in which saints have proverbially been tempted, a beautiful woman. Modestly she called upon him one day, told him " that she has long had a more than ordinary Value for my Ministry," that she was charmed with his " person, to such a Degree, that she could not but break in upon me, with her moſt importunate Requeſt, that I would make her mine. . . . " Nor was this " polite Gentlewoman " merely enamored of the person of the handsome widower. He meant to her earthly love, and more; " the higheſt Consideration she had in it was her eternal Salvation, for if she were mine, she could not but hope the Effeɗ of it would be, that she should also be Chriſt's." The wily young lady was something of a psychologiſt. She was not bothered by the miniſter's " way of living, in continued Prayers, Tears, Faſts, and macerating Devotions and Reservations "; such religious exercises made the prospeɗ of life with him the more romantic. He felt that the " Dispensations of Heaven " toward him in the death of his lovely consort had been " very awful." Here was a woman anyone might covet. He set a great value upon her and her "incomparable accomplishments." In faɗ she was probably the firſt witty woman with whom he had ever conversed. His wife had been under sixteen when he courted and married her; during their sixteen years together it is doubtful if he had ever had time or occasion aɗually to converse with her save on personal matters. His intelleɗual life lay in his ſtudy and among men. Now for the firſt time he met a clever woman with conversational powers, one who could talk with him of things other than the material or spiritual necessities of a household. He was equally fascinated by her wit and her flattery. How to deal with her was a problem; his inclinations obviously led him to consider favoring her requeſt; how delightful a thing to have conſtantly by him one so charming, so amusing, so trusting, and to feel that while he enjoyed her companionship, he was leading her to God. She was only twenty, a highly desirable damsel. But on the other hand he knew she had been " a very aiery Person " whose reputation had been " under some Disadvantage." There were snares in this " odd Matter," it was clear. There was but one answer: " how could my Lord Jesus Christ Himself treat a returning Sinner? " It was not for Cotton Mather to refuse help to a lamb, a beautiful lamb, returning to the fold.

" Nature itself causes in me," he reflected, " a mighty Tenderness for a person so very amiable. Breeding requires me to treat her with Honour and Respect, and very much of Deference, to all that she shall at any time ask of me. But Religion, above all, obliges me, instead of a rash rejecting her Conversation, to contrive rather, how I may imitate the Goodness of the Lord Jesus Christ, in his Dealing with such as are upon a Conversion with Him." He made cautious inquiries about her. Was it only his troubling widowhood that made her seem so alluring? No; everybody with admiration confessed her to be, " for her charming Accomplishments, an incomparable Person. . . . " But, alas! a " violent Storm of Opposition " came; her father's house admitted the wrong people and his congregation doubted her discretion. And yet she was so very lovely.

There was but one thing to do. Dear to him as she had become, hard for him as his widowhood was, dearer to him and harder to part with was his usefulness, the greatest of all his passions. If he continued in this affair he realized that his usefulness would be seriously impaired if not ended. He muſt therefore resolutely break off this courtship. In a letter to the seductive girl he begged that he " might not be kill'd by hearing any more of it." Yet such was his " flexible Tenderness, as to be conquered by the Importunities of several, to allow some further Interviews." He confessed to his diary that he was " a moſt miserable man." Nevertheless he was ſtern; he would endure her company, but he would talk of nothing but religion. So he " did with all the Charms [he] could imagine, draw that witty Gentlewoman into tearful Expressions of her Consent, unto all the Articles in the Covenant of Grace, the Articles of her Marriage and Union with the Great L[ord] Redeemer." But the young lady's hopes were obviously not dashed so long as his conversation retained the language of courtship though now it was the erotic symbolism of Chriſtianity.

And now there came upon him all the forces of evil in full panoply: temptations, delusions, and " Vexations from Satan." His troubled mind could not reſt. Kept awake all night, he supposed that his vigil was due to a wreſtling with the Lord for his great congregation. He thought of the boys and girls of his flock and prayed especially for them. But prayer and vigil gave little balm for his " doleful Disconsolations." His relatives took an extreme diſtaſte for the " aiery " girl, feared his over-valuing her, and treated him with " unsupportable Strangeness and Harshness."

It became necessary to set the " diſtressing Affayr " before God. And " the ingenious Child, that solicits my

[191]

Respects unto her, I cry to the Lord with Fervency and
Agony and Floods of Tears, that she may be the Lord's;
and that her Union and Marriage to the Lord Jesus
Christ, may be the Effect of the Discourses I have had
with her. But I also resign her and offer her up unto the
Lord."

If Cotton Mather was for God, the lovely, amiable,
and witty girl was for God in him. And fast after fast
increased rather than quenched his flames.

Now, worst of all, in another week Boston had the
story. And all possible talk of virtuous carriage and notorious conversion would not wash white the damsel's
sullied reputation. Moreover, gossip, with a " mighty
Noise," had it that poor Cotton Mather, who aimed only
at " Conformity to . . . Jesus Christ, and Serviceableness
to Him " was engaged in a purely mundane courtship.
Her addresses obviously had to be rejected lest his " Usefulness be horribly Ruined," but it was only because the
Lord's name would suffer that she was rejected. He made
the sacrifice cheerfully, he hoped, " tho' she be so very
charming a Person." He took to prayer feeling that his
" Victory over Flesh and Blood " was no " unhappy
Symptom " of his soul's regeneration; and he reminded
the Lord that he believed that he should " one Day meet
with some wonderful Recompences." He prayed, too,
that God would preserve the lady, ejaculating " but I
must continue praying for her! "

Though he had now struck his Knife into the Heart
of his Sacrifice " by a Letter to her Mother," his mind
was not relieved. The Devil continued to tempt him hor-

ribly. " Sometimes, Temptations to *Impurities;* and sometimes to Blasphemy, and Atheism, and the Abandonment of all Religion, as a meer Delusion; and sometimes, to self-Deſtruction itself." To overcome these bitter thoughts common to all disappointed lovers — though in this case the disappointment was self-inflicted — Mather turned to prayer. He decided that it might be the moſt honorable course for him to remain " all the reſt of my little Time, in an unspotted Widowhood." However, his " flexible Temper " yielded to his father's repeated persuasions that he remarry. It was not mere idle words for him to say that he could not easily resiſt his father's exhortations. Though he was now forty, his relationship with his father was little different from that of twenty years earlier. Filial piety was the guiding ſtar of his life.

He turned more heavily to prayer. Gossip multiplied, misrepresenting him and his " coarse, tho' juſt " treatment of the alluring damsel. His friends urged him to put a ſtop to the whole matter by marrying some one else. He had already faſted and prayed much for guidance in this diſtressful widowhood; now he felt that he muſt do something extraordinary, something which had probably not been done " by any Man living in the World." This was a three-day faſt, a ſtrain on the vitality of even a much ſtronger man. " The great Point of my Return to the *married State,* I did on each of the three Dayes, with a Variety of tearful Supplications plead before the Lord. I have submitted unto all the Inconveniences of a *single State,* if the Lord will confine me to it; only I have

[193]

begg'd of Him, the Gifts of Purity and Patience. But I have left the Matter entirely unto the Lord; . . . I have committed unto my Lord Jesus Christ, the Care of providing an agreeable Consort for me. . . . I know, that some surprising Thing will be done for me." This prolonged fast, however, left him in a low state of mind which was somewhat corrected by constant demands for his services as preacher and by flattering requests for the publication of his sermons. The next fast was postponed a week lest his health be injured; and on this day he was assured that a " desireable Consort " would be found for him by " a glorious Angel of the Lord . . . (as for *Isaac*) of old." Since he could not write a lyric for the lovely lady whom he was endeavoring to forget, he turned his poetical yearnings in another direction, writing a poem for young people that would capture their hearts " and *make* them to become the Lord's."

His officious friends reawakened gossip and made him exceedingly unhappy by attempting to arrange what they considered a suitable match for him. But though he came near yielding he felt that the Lord had not yet sufficiently directed him. Another day of fast was in order. This time the unhappiness vanished in ecstasies. He came near swooning under the insupportable raptures of these assurances of divine love.

But the peace and security thus gained, the relieving of sexual tension in religious fervor, were quickly disturbed by the renewed attentions of the fascinating young lady. She with her mother came to his father, Increase Mather, charming " the Neighbours into her Interests " and renewing her importunities. Cotton Mather was not, however, to be flattered out of his fixed resolution to do nothing that could possibly harm " the holy Interests of Religion." He feared equally that she might by his refusal come to some mischief, and that his chances of finding a wife elsewhere might be injured by a renewed burst of gossip.

To strengthen his resolution he held another fast day, and a week later another, having been sorely tempted; and again the next week another, this last because of the gossip now maliciously attributing to him dishonorable conduct in his relations with the young woman. What the imagination of Boston could make of the affair is shown in the pamphlet issued by Dudley and his friends three years later: " The story is this: A Gentlewooman of *Gayety,* near *Boston,* was frequently visited by the Reverend Mr. *C. M.* which giving offence to some of his Audience, he promised to avoid her Conversation. But *Good* intentions being frustrated by *Vicious* Inclinations, he beomes again her humble Servant; this *Reciprocal* promise being first made, that NEITHER OF THEM SHOULD CONFESS THEIR SEEING EACH OTHER: However, it becoming again publick, his Father accused him of it, who after two or three HEMS to recover himself, (like Col. *Partridge* at the Council-Board) gave this *Aequivocal* Answer, INDEED, FATHER, IF I SHOULD SAY I DID SEE HER, I SHOULD TELL A GREAT LYE. This is the Gentleman distinguishable for his *Character. . . .*"

Mather's politial enemies in thus bringing to life an old bit of gossip, naturally omitted to state that both the gentlewoman and her mother, in spite of their pain over his decision, came to Mather's defense, asserting that far from doing any unworthy thing, he had " acted most honourably and religiously towards them, and as became a Christian, and a Minister "; and that they looked upon " Mr. M —— r *to be as great a saint of God, as any upon earth.*"

As " an exemplary *Revenge* upon the *Divel* " both for tempting him and for stirring up impertinent stories about him, Cotton Mather with, however, a real fear that perhaps the devil's rage would get him even as he preached, entertained the townspeople and those who came in from the country to Thursday lecture with a discourse, the first of a series, all highly detailed, on *The Wiles of the Divel.*

The defeated gentlewoman was not, however, silenced. She made a great clamour when she realized that he meant to hold to his decision against her; and when the Lord after his repeated prayers directed Cotton Mather to an amiable gentlewoman within two houses of his own, a gentlewoman of " Piety and Probity, and with a most unspotted Reputation," the rage of the rejected lady " of so rare a Witt, but so little Grace " was cyclonic. Her threats astonished the poor man; he was for once left speechless. He could only leave her and turn to prayer. He felt that the danger threatened not him alone, but Christ's very self. He reminded the Lord that His name would suffer if a servant of His were permitted to be so buffeted. He reminded Him that He could if He chose conquer Satan; and to Him he delivered over the misguided young woman with all her threats. Within a few days his prayers were answered; the young lady of her own accord sent him a letter recanting her threats and promising to leave him in peace. Upon this his court-ship of his neighbour went on " with pure, chaft, noble Strokes, and the Smiles of God upon it."

III

This lady was about thirty years old, having been left a widow not long after marriage four years earlier. Her firft husband, Richard Hubbard, had been a mariner; her father, now dead, a Dr. John Clark. She was therefore " Honourably descended and related "; and seems to have been endowed with all due housewifely virtues besides those of " good Witt and Sense." Moreover, she was " a very comely person." She had one child, a son about the same age as Cotton Mather's son Increase. Since, he recorded, he had often urged his former wife to adopt a fatherless child that God might bless his children there-for, he could hardly objeft to educating this child in return for all the services its mother would do for his children. He found her abundantly agreeable; and prep-arations hurried on so that the marriage occurred one month and four days after his firft visit to her and seven months after the death of his firft wife. As the marriage came in the evening, he spent the entire day in Thanks-giving for having at laft come " to the rich Harveft of my Prayers, my Tears, my Resignations."

On the following day he preached the Thursday lefture to a vaft assembly, naïvely recording that as he had

" never declined any Service unto the Lord, for any Affliction, so neither should I for any Enjoyment."

The bride's brother gave a handsome entertainment, and five days later Cotton Mather made " an agreeable Entertainment at my House, for the Relatives of both." His time was now much interrupted. Friends called to offer congratulations; and he found the company of his new wife delightful. He feared left his " *Prosperity* prove a Disadvantage . . . and left a sensual, casual, insipid Frame of Spirit " grow upon him.

The serious illness of three children hardly made a pause in these joyous months crowded with activity that spread itself over poems on the death of virtuous ladies, tracts for the Christianizing of Indians, and a general circumventing of the wiles of the devil, whose evil presence he forever suspected, especially at those times when he was inclined to be most happy. The severe winter made him think of the sufferings of the poor, in contrast to his comforts, and he redoubled his charities. In the spring his heart overflowed with especial gratitude because he saw not only himself, but his neighbours and the very birds and beasts happy in various delights. He could not believe in unadulterated joy, but all he could with soul-searching find to lament was the want of good servants in his family.

In time the usual adversities of life came to restore the balance of daily life; he himself was ill, finally conquering a distressing cough by prayer and fasting. There was always for him a somewhat morbid curiosity to see just how far he could abuse his frail body. He had the gambler's joy in taking a risk, the risks being not of gold, but of health. Hence at times when he was almoſt sure that he could not endure physical privation he would hold a faſt, watching the results upon himself with a valetudinarian intereſt. Now, too, his relatives showed themselves as " hardly to be matched in all *New England* for their Wickedness," the two chief offenders being his former wife's brother and his ſiſter Hannah's husband. Hannah, " a moſt ingenious and . . . good-carriaged Child," was " married unto a raving Brute. The Fellow, whom they called her Husband, perfectly murdered her, by his base, and abusive Way of treating her; and he chose to employ in a special manner, the Ebullitions of his Venome " againſt the brother she " loved dearly." Her death in spite of his prayers to ease it was " long, and hard." From it her brother extracted what satisfaction he could; he felt that she had cause to bless the wretch, her husband, in that because of him she had become " a serious and gracious Chriſtian, weaned from this World, and fitted for a better."

Occasionally in these years of ſtrife and disappointment in political and Harvard hopes, he was assailed with religious doubt, at one time being moved to write: " I have been lately Tempted with a *new Assault* from Hell, violently made upon me. I am assaulted with Sollicitations to look upon the whole *Chriſtian Religion,* as — (I dare not mention, what!)" From these doubts he escaped by fervent prayer and reflections on the paths of usefulness. And in general the years settled down to the humdrum routine of lectures and sermons; and at home the births and deaths of children. His lack of financial acumen, added to the increasing size of his family, led him in 1709 into such poverty that not only he himself, but two of his children, were " *cloathed with Rags,*" a state of poverty which he thought was not to be lamented since it brought him in " conformity to . . . Lord JESUS CHRIST." With the Dudley fight quiescent there seemed nothing more pressing to sharpen his wits upon. He looked inward and invented what he could not know would become the future practice of Boy Scouts the world over. This was his scheme for " *Devices of Good* " one for each day of the week. From now on his diary was sprinkled with G. D.'s (good devised or good devices).

IV

The great event of 1710 was the honor of the degree of Doctor of Divinity bestowed upon him by the University of Glasgow. Foreign recognition of New Englanders was not so common as to fail to stir up envy and malice. Harvard, now wholly out of the hands of the Mathers and their party, had paid no attention to the scholarly achievements of this prominent alumnus; even if it had had the right to bestow honorary degrees, it would not have singled out a Mather. This attention from a foreign university was quickly seized upon by his enemies, who rejoiced and doubtless helped in the appearance of a scurrilous poem ON C. MR's. DIPLOMA:

The mad enthusiast, thirsting after fame,
By endless volum'ns thought to raise a name.

With undigested trash he throngs the Press;
Thus striving to be greater he's the less,

.   .   .   .

. . . — Parkhurst says, *Satis fecisti,*
My belly's full of your Magnalia Christi.
Your crude Divinity and History
Will not with a censorious age agree.

.   .   .   .

Daz'd with the stol'n title of his Sire,
To be a Doctor he is all afire.

.   .   .   .

To Britain's Northern Clime in haste he sends,
And begs an independent boon from Presbyterian friends;
Rather than be without, he'd beg it of the Fiends.
Facetious George brought him this Libertie
To write C. Mather first and then D.D. "

For once, their usual sides reversed, Increase Mather
took up the cudgels for his son. Judge Sewall noted:
" Dr. Increase Mather lays before me the first Libel, the
Copy being of Sam. Sewall's [the judge's son?] writing;
and mentions Mr. Bromfield, for me to consult with
what to doe." Sewall took prompt action, summoning
the author John Banister and publisher Aaron Stuckey
three days later. " Mr. Tho. Brattle came of himself and
pleaded much in favour of the Libellers . . . and against
the injured Doctors. . . . Mr. Brattle argued hard." Perhaps Banister was another Calef, a tool for his use. But
the judge was not moved; he had a letter from Cotton
Mather himself urging clemency for Banister. In the face

of this magnanimity on the part of the injured man, Brattle's advocacy did not smell sweet; Sewall for this reason " invited him not to Dinner." Deciding to take a middle course, he fined Baniſter twenty shillings for this and a second libel, perhaps that about the gentle-woman of gayety; and the publisher twenty shillings for the one he published, binding both over for good behavior.

Sewall's paſtor, Pemberton, had been invited to dinner; and he now demanded an account of the matter. Ebenezer Pemberton was a fiery man. He had shortly before this, at a time when wheat was scarce and dear, objeſted violently to a shipment of " about 6000 Bushels besides Bread " saying in answer to Sewall's mild remark that God pitied and helped even those who " brought themselves into Straits by their own fault," that " They were not God's people but the Devil's people that wanted Corn. There was Corn to be had; if they had not impoverish'd themselves by Rum, they might buy Corn." The reverend gentleman obviously objeſted to tightening his belt that the improvident might be fed. At this time he went on to upbraid the judge " that he was invited to Diñer, and then not sent for at Diñertime; was sick with waiting; loſt his own Diñer; knew not where we din'd; 'twas indecent to ly lurking at the ordinary; wanted not a Diñer." Here was an adversary whose tongue was sharper than the Mathers' own; one wonders that he did not furnish keener barbs for Baniſter's libels. Now his wrath over the Mathers' mild viſtory in the fining of Baniſter seethed; in the absence of the Mathers he poured it over the judge who had seemingly upheld them. " Mr. Pemberton with extraordinary Vehemency said, (capering with his feet) If the Mathers order'd it, I would shoot him thorow. I told him he was in a passion. He said he was not in a Passion. I said it was so much the worse. He said the Fire from the Altar was equally impartial. Upbraiding me, very plainly, as I underſtood it, with Partiality. The President said, The Governour was barbarously treated (meaning Dr. Cotton Mather's Letter to his Excellency). I answered; That was put to the Council. Mr. Mayhew told me afterward, that I said his Carriage was neither becoming a Scholar nor Miniſter. The Truth is I was surpris'd to see my self insulted with such extraordinary Fierceness, by my Paſtor, juſt when I had been vindicating two worthy Embassadors of Chriſt (his own usual Phrase) from moſt villanous Libels." After dinner as they walked in the ſtreet in spite of Sewall's proteſt againſt such publicity, Pemberton returned to the challenge, fishing up an old grievance that he might seem an injured person with the Mathers preferred in his place. He said that " Capt. Martin, the Com̄adore, had abus'd him, yet I took no notice of it: I answer'd, you never laid it before me. He said, You knew it. I said, I knew it not. (For every Rumor is not ground sufficient for a Juſtice of Peace to proceed upon; and Mr. Pemberton never spake word of it to me before.) He said Capt. Martin call'd him Rascal in the Street, and said had it not been for his coat, he would have cân'd him." And then Captain Martin was invited to dine with the superior court so that Pemberton couldn't go. Further the Council, taking little note of Martin's abuse of him, invited Martin " to their Treat at the Return from Annapolis Royal." Sewall unwilling to deny Pemberton his right to anger, noted for his own satisfaction that " Tis difficult medling with Captains of Frigats. Reasons of State require the overlooking many grievous Things."

His ardor dimmed by his fine, John Banister was not moved to satirize Cotton Mather's next honor from abroad in 1713, and it was not until 1720 that the Brattles could stir up a scandal about it. This was the very real honor of election to the Royal Society. Perhaps one reason for the silence of the Brattles was that a similar honor was bestowed on William Brattle in the following year, so that his envy was thereby quieted.

According to custom, Cotton Mather was first asked if he would care to be proposed as a member after he had, by request, submitted several letters on the natural history of New England. The secretary of the society informed him first of the proposal of his name, then of his election, whereupon not only he but the Royal Society publications attached F.R.S. to his name. The fact that the rules of the society required the ceremony of investiture within four weeks of election (though this period might be lengthened; and indeed would have to be for one overseas) gave to his enemies a loophole for the attacks some years later.

Now, however, Cotton Mather could write a letter of thanks to the secretary and gracefully arrive at the always embarrassing matter of dues: " I must further pray you to be my Instructor, (for, S^r, you must imagine that you have now a sort of tame Indian under your Tuition) what the Rules of my Relation will oblige me to observe, in ye point of those little pecuniary Expenses, wth which I am to consider ye Treasurer of ye Society."

The *Curiosa Americana* which he had already submitted and those he was to submit in the years that followed were not unlike those contributed by the members in England. In the current state of science anything curious, remarkable, illustrious, or memorable was open to investigation. When these things were attested by men whose reputation for veracity was undoubted, men of science would indeed have been bigoted not to take notice of them. Not to believe in the incredible is an untenable creed for science if it is to progress. Much of the mechanism of our modern world has sprung from man's desire to accomplish the impossible. So Cotton Mather, who had previously scoffed at mermaids and mermen, felt that he had to give credence to the tale of " three honorable and credible " eye-witnesses who, " coming in a Boat from *Milford* to *Brainford* " saw " a Creature that seem'd a *Man*, lying on the Top of a Rock." It evaded capture, and " Jump'd off ye Rock, & with all Possible Expedition flounced into the Water." They described this Triton fully, having seen " his *Head*, and *Face*, and *Neck*, and *Shoulders*, & *Arms*, and *Elbows*, and *Breast*, and *Back*, all of an *Humane Shape*, only his *Arms*, were little more than half the Length of a Mans. He wanted not for *Hair*, which was of a *Grayish* Colour. However, — *desinit in piscem*; His Lower Parts were those of a *Fish*, and Coloured like a *Mackarel*. His Tail was forked,

and he had Two Fins about half a Foot above yᵉ Tail.
The whole Animal was about Five or Six Foot in Length."
Certainly this deserved investigation in any age.

The first thirteen letters dealt with various subjects.
Naturally the Indians were interesting objects of investigation — the man whose daughter was destined to be
Cotton Mather's third wife had whole sheafs of questions
hurled at him by an English physician on the characteristics and physical habits of the Indians. Cotton Mather
was particularly interested in such things as their use of
plants in medicines and in the Indians' division of time
into sleeps, moons, and winters. Earthquakes, lightning,
and rattlesnakes are dealt with in this series of communi-
cations, as are also monstrous births and other obstetric
curiosities. Perhaps the most interesting was the first
letter which gave an extract from his gigantic work,
Biblia Americana, of the discovery of teeth and bones
found beyond Albany at Clavarack. These seemed to be
the remains of one of the giants of other days. The Indians
had a tradition about this giant, named Maughkompos,
who lived upon fish, eating four sturgeons for so light
a meal as breakfast. Here is an early example of the tall
tale grown big in America. Excerpts from these letters
were printed in the society's official organ in 1714 and
there Cotton Mather had the pleasure of seeing his name
printed with F.R.S. after it.

The honor of his election to the Royal Society was particularly gratifying at this time when the town was filled
with " riotous Young Men " who " On purpose to insult
Piety " would come under Mather's window late at night

and " sing profane and filthy Songs," taking clubs from
his woodpile to attack those who tried to stop them.

v

Such irritations were, however, as nothing to the
calamities coming. An epidemic of measles attacked Boston, which Mather hoped, as he comforted the afflicted,
would pass by his household where another child was
expected. About the middle of October his son Increase
fell ill, but recovered, living to cause his father much
greater sorrow. A week later the daughter Nibby was
taken ill, and a few days later Katy. Mrs. Mather, having
attended the sick children diligently, gave birth somewhat
prematurely to twins, a boy and a girl. Two days later
not only she but the remaining three daughters were
all ill, as well as a maidservant. The cup offered Mather
by the Lord seemed very bitter indeed; he held a fast
day to obtain pardon for whatever sins of his had been
responsible for this weight of calamity, and if possible,
life for his wife and children. As his wife grew weaker
he felt that his supplications to the Lord must have somehow lacked fervency, that they had " a most unaccountable Death and Damp upon them! " He strove to make
himself and his " dear Consort " resigned. " God made
her willing to Dy. God extinguished in her the Fear of
Death." Her husband gave himself up to consoling her
and preparing her to meet God. On the day she died " in
the midst of his Sorrowes and Hurries, the Lord helped
[him] to praepare no less than two Sermons, for a public
Thanksgiving, which [was] to be celebrated " the twelfth

[207]

of November. The next day he preached and prepared for publication her funeral sermon; and his erſtwhile enemy Pemberton was among the bearers. In this time of woe with his children ſtill ill, he could yet look into his heart and find reasons for thankfulness unto the Lord; his life and a fair degree of health and several children had so far been preserved, all comfortably provided for; his reputation had been recognized abroad; he was miniſter of a large and prosperous church; and he was on the beſt of terms with God. He felt that there was further reason for being thankful in that after " so many Hurries and Sorrowes, and grievous Disadvantages," he could ſtill feel cheerful and grateful and at one with the Lord.

The maidservant's death did not diſturb this frame of mind, for this " wild, vain, airy Girl " after her coming into his family had been led by him to religion, and had been baptized by him. He felt that he muſt make the misfortunes of his family an example of piety to the world. But when his pet, the little Jerusha, grew worse, he could but pray, " *Father, Lett that Cup pass from me. Nevertheless —* " Resignation in this case was very hard; Jerusha had been an exceptionally bright child, dear to her father for her cleverness and her piety; now at two and a half she lay speechless for hours, reviving only to say " *That she would go to Jesus Chriſt.*" The day of her death was the day of the funeral of the twins whose birth had so shortly preceded their mother's death. The loss of this child seems to have been the greateſt grief of this trying time.

Her father felt that he muſt turn his sorrow into attention toward his remaining children, and ſtrictly oversee their education and their table manners. Moreover, he muſt give an example to the town of " not Fainting in the Day of Adversity." At the public lecture on Thursday he was the speaker; the calamities in his family would naturally turn the " Eyes of the People " much upon him. As a public man he could not give way to his woe.

Cotton Mather suſtained the loss of two wives with grief, to be sure, but with no tender feelings. It is obvious that his wives were in no way companions; at leaſt in his diary there is nothing to indicate that with either of them he ever conversed in a friendly way. He did note his intentions of asking them to follow the prevailing cuſtom of taking notes on sermons, that their notes, as became a divine's wife, might be fuller than ordinary people's; and his recurring determination to speak more piously in their presence. He felt that whenever he was near his wife he ought somehow to make his speech memorable and improving. This is the attitude of a teacher, not of a companion. Hence at their deaths there is none of the tenderness expressed in a letter such as this:

" Dear Sister

" I am at length Come to the Sad Task of mentioning to you the departure of my dear Wife, the Sole partner of all my felicity in this Life, which has left so many tender Impressions on my poor heart that wherever I turne my Selfe mind or Body my heart ever Sickens with

[209]

some Soft Ideas of Her footsteps, but I desire to be dumb & Silent as it was the Will of God, who has taken Her to Himselfe, & was pleased to give Her Such measures of His Grace under all the Tryals He called Her to as was greatly Edifying to all about Her. Her dolorous pains for nights & Dayes without intermission, without sleep, put me in Constant terrour that it must distract Her, but God Supported Her Wonderfully with a Clear understanding to the last moment, with a humble submission to His Will. Her Soul Sustained it all, but the Body Dyed — God grant us equal Supports in the Day of Tryal."

Here is every sign of human grief — the heart ever sickening with "Soft Idea of Her Footsteps," even the capitalizing of every "Her" showing how dear this woman was to her husband. This man missed his wife's presence in a way incomprehensible to Cotton Mather. Mather felt the loss of both his wives sincerely; but it was the loss merely of a housekeeper and of a bedfellow that he lamented.

He noted pathetically in his diary: "My glorious Lord has not only brought me into a State of widowhood, but I must also look upon myself, as obliged unto a Continuance in that State, all the rest of my little Time in this World; And this after I have been very agreeably circumstanced in the married State. I must now, not only quicken, and most religiously observe, a Rule heretofore practised with me, that if an impure Thought start into my Mind, I must presently reject it, and rebuke it, and

make it a Provocation to form an holy Thought in Con-
tradiction to it: but also, I must with the most heavenly
Methods of Meditation, Supplication, and Resolution,
endeavour to obtain from Heaven, the Grace of the most
unspotted Purity."

CHAPTER SEVEN

"The Diseases of my soul are not cured until I
arrive to the most unspotted Chastitie and Puritie."
— *Diary of Cotton Mather*

I

BY 1714 Boston's population had grown to about twelve thousand. The largeſt and moſt important town in North America, it was more varied and cosmopolitan than it had been fifty years before, in Cotton Mather's childhood; it was changing with the eighteenth century, that century of clashing contradictions which is all things to all hiſtorians. But with its growth it had loſt that vigorous independence of character that makes seventeenth-century Boſton vivid and picturesque even to those who bitterly hate its moſt characteriſtic qualities. There is something in narrowness and bigotry reinforced by gallows and whipping poſt which mere provinciality cannot possess. There is a touch of the heroic in the roll of drums summoning the populace to the uprising that imprisoned Andros and Dudley and triumphantly demanded the disarmament of the royal frigate in the harbor, that is lacking in the sordid conflict of Assembly and governor over a mere matter of salary. The witchcraft excitement assumed a lamentable onslaught upon the army of God by the hoſts of the devil, but the excitement over paper money merely involved a lamentable ignorance of economics. When Anne Hutchinson and Roger Williams disagreed with religious leaders they had a trial which today rings with life, and a banishment which makes of them heroic figures in American history; when the members of the New North

VIEW OF BOSTON, 1743

Church quarrelled with their minister, Mr. Thacher, and with each other, splitting in 1718 to form the New Brick Church, they appear merely as provincial clowns. " The aggrieved Brethren went off in bad humor," says a contemporary, " and proceeded to the gathering of another Church. In the plenitude of zeal, they first thought of denominating it the Revenge Church of Christ. . . . They placed the figure of a *Cock* as a vane upon the steeple, out of derision to Mr. Thacher [minister of the New North] whose Christian name was *Peter.* Taking advantage of a wind which turned the head of

[213]

the Cock towards the New North when it was placed upon the spindle, a merry fellow straddled over it and crowed three times, to complete the ceremony."

To Increase Mather whom Benjamin Franklin remembered " sitting in an easy chair, apparently very old and feeble," whose boyhood knew the grave men of God who had sailed in the *Arabella,* and whose prime knew royalty at the court of King James," such clowning must have seemed a desecration fit to bring down fire from heaven. It is not strange that a few years later a fast day was appointed " for the younger generation."

This younger generation that stood in the need of prayer and fasting was to provide the elder statesmen of the great Revolution. Among them was Benjamin Franklin whose father was a devout adherent of the Old South Church and whom Sewall suggested as a fit man to set the tune for the psalm-singing, partly because " The Return of the Gallery where Mr. Franklin sat was a place very Convenient for it." Free thinker as he was, Benjamin Franklin always remembered Cotton Mather with respect. When he was an old man he wrote to Samuel Mather, Cotton's son: "When I was a boy, I met with a book, entitled *Essays to do Good,* which I think was written by your father. It had been so little regarded by a former possessor, that several leaves of it were torn out; but the remainder gave me such a turn of thinking, as to have influence on my conduct through life; for I have always set a greater value on the character of a *doer of good,* than on any other kind of reputation; and if I have been, as you seem to think, a useful citizen, the public owes the advantage of it to that book. . . . It is more than sixty years since I left Boston, but I remember well both your father and grandfather, having heard them both in the pulpit, and seen them in their houses. The last time I saw your father was in the beginning of 1724, when I visited him after my first trip to Pennsylvania. He received me in his library, and on my taking leave showed me a shorter way out of the house through a narrow passage, which was crossed by a beam over head. We were still talking as I withdrew, he accompanying me behind, and I turning partly towards him, when he said hastily, ' *Stoop, stoop!* ' I did not understand him, till I felt my head hit against the beam. He was a man that never missed any occasion of giving instruction, and upon this he said to me, ' *You are young, and have the world before you;* STOOP *as you go through it, and you will miss many hard thumps.*' This advice, thus beat into my head, has frequently been of use to me; and I often think of it, when I see pride mortified, and misfortunes brought upon people by their carrying their heads too high."

Despite Benjamin Franklin's kind memories, the Mathers had unpleasant experiences with his brother, the publisher of Boston's third regular newspaper, the *New England Courant* which first appeared in 1721, when " The contests and discussions in the government rose to a greater height than they had done since the religious feuds in the years 1636 and 1637. . . . There was a general cry for want of money, and yet the bills of credit, which were the only money, were daily de-

[215]

preciating. The depreciation was grievous to all creditors, but particularly distressing to the clergy and other salary men, to widows and orphans whose estates consisted of money at interest, perhaps just enough to support them, and being reduced to one half the former value, they found themselves on a sudden in a state of poverty and want. . . . By these calamities, the minds of the people were prepared for impressions from pamphlets, courants, and other news-papers, which were frequently published, in order to convince them that their civil liberties and privileges were struck at, and that a general union was necessary." Franklin's newspaper, assisted by a group of writers which a contemporary paper likens to the " Hell Fire Club " of London, specialized in attacks upon the clergy. They drew from Cotton Mather the resolution to give " warnings . . . unto the wicked Printer, and his Accomplices, who every week publish a vile Paper to lessen and blacken the Ministers of the Town, and render their Ministry ineffectual.

" A Wickedness never parallel'd any where upon the Face of the Earth! "

II

Throughout his life Cotton Mather felt that he was being attacked and abused from every side. In 1721 he noted: " A Lieutenant of a Man of War, whom I am a Stranger to, designing to putt an Indignity upon me, has called his *Negro-Slave* by the Name of COTTON MATHER." Earlier he had written: " It is a Law with me, that when Abuses are offered me, I be awakened unto some agreeable Improvement in Piety upon them." His forgiving spirit was grievously tried as he grew older and more aware of a changing world where ministers no longer sat in seats of power. " One of the first Things which the Pyrates," he noted in 1724, " who are now so much the *Terror of them that haunt the Sea,* impose on their poor Captives, is: *To curse Dr. M——.*" But Dr. M—— had a holy revenge for, he continued: " The Pyrates now strangely fallen into the Hands of Justice here, make me *the first Man,* whose Visits and Councils and Prayers they beg for. Some of them under Sentence of Death, chuse to hear from me, the last Sermon they hear in the World."

The thorn of Harvard College naturally pricked him most deeply. After Leverett's inauguration as president in 1708 both Increase and Cotton Mather refused to take any share in its government, Cotton attending but one meeting of the overseers, and his father none, in Leverett's presidency. When Cotton Mather received his degree of Doctor of Divinity from Glasgow, Leverett had his doubts about recognizing it in the new catalogue of graduates because of Mather's " undutiful " letter to Governor Dudley. The choleric Mr. Pemberton, called into conference, presented the matter to the governor, who showed a proper Christian spirit, saying " that he would not have the said President to omit inserting the title on his account."

When in 1718 a graduate named Pierpont was refused his master's degree because of charges " of contemning, reproaching, and insulting the government of the College, and particularly the tutors, for their management in admission of scholars," Pierpont defied the college by entering a suit at law to compel the corporation to give him his degree. Cotton Mather naturally assumed that Pierpont was in the right and wrote to Governor Shute in behalf of the " abused and oppressed " ſtudent. " Though the College be under a very unhappy government," he wrote, " yett for my own part I earneſtly desire, that it may go on as easily and as quietly as possible. *And your Excellency's incomparable goodness and wisdom will easily discern and approve the intentions used in this letter, and leave it and it's writer covered under the darkeſt concealment.* And the rather, because (for some reason) I desire to keep at the greateſt diſtance imaginable from all the affairs of Harvard."

But he could no more keep at a diſtance than any prominent alumnus has ever been able to do, especially since his son Samuel received his bachelor's degree in 1723. In that year the overseers voted " that a visitation of the College would very much serve the intereſts of religion and learning in that society " and proposed an inquiry which would bring joy to the souls of Fundamentaliſts today. Moſt of the " articles " which they proposed showed clearly enough the fear that under Leverett the ſtudents' souls might not be the firſt consideration. " What are the books in Divinity which are moſt used, and more particularly recommended to the ſtudents.

" How are the Saturday exercises performed, and are the great concerns of their souls duly inculcated on the youth.

" What is the state of the College as to the morals of the youth.

" Whether the Holy Scriptures be daily read in the Hall, and how often expounded.

" Whether the tutors and students do duly give their attendance on the public prayers and reading of the Holy Scriptures in the Hall, morning and evening.

.   .   .   .

" How the Lord's day is observed, and the public duties of it attended by that society."

To help the committee, Cotton Mather drew up, on his own account, a draft of " Important points relating to the education at Harvard College needful to be inquired into." These points charged that there had been " a sensible and notorious decay " of " solid learning," that the speaking of Latin had been " discountenanced," that " the Tutors often make the pupils get by heart a deal of insipid stuff and trash, that they bid them at the same time to believe nothing of it," that " the books mostly read among them are . . . plays, novels, empty and vicious pieces of poetry, and even Ovid's Epistles, which have a vile tendency to corrupt good manners," and finally, most modern charge of all, that " many godly persons in the country have . . . with sad hearts lamented it, that their children, who have left their families with some Gospel symptoms of piety upon them, after they came to live at College, do quickly lose all, and neither do nor hear any more such things as they had before they went from home." It is clear that godly young

[219]

Samuel Mather, the last and only dull Mather of the line, had been telling tales out of school.

There was something of triumph for Cotton Mather in the speedy report of the overseers that among other derelictions of the college, " although there is a considerable number of virtuous and studious youth in the College, yet there has been a practice of several immoralities; particularly stealing, lying, idleness, picking of locks, and too frequent use of strong drink; which immoralities, it is feared, still continue in the College, notwithstanding the faithful endeavours of the rulers of the House to suppress them."

When, therefore, President Leverett died suddenly in 1724, Cotton Mather might well believe that an orthodox minister of wide reputation for learning, a doctor of divinity, and a Fellow of the Royal Society, would be the obvious choice for the place. And apparently many others believed so, too. But the corporation was of a different mind. In the bitterness of despair Cotton Mather confided to his diary: " I am informed that yesterday the six men who call themselves the Corporation of the College met, and, contrary to the epidemical expectation of the country, chose a modest young man, of whose piety (and little else) every one gives a laudable character. I always foretold these two things of the Corporation; first, that if it were possible for them to steer clear of me, they will do so; secondly, that, if it were possible for them to act foolishly, they will do so.

" The perpetual envy *with which my essays to serve the kingdom of God are treated among them, and the*

[220]

dread that Satan has of my beating up his quarters at the College, led me into the former sentiment;* the marvellous indiscretion, with which the affairs of the College are managed, led me into the latter."

Cotton Mather was too closely connected with his father for the Corporation to look upon him with favor; having once wrested the college from the father, they were not likely to deliver it over to the son. When Joseph Sewall, the " modest young man," declined the office, as did also Benjamin Colman of the Brattle Church, Benjamin Wadsworth of the First Church of Boston was duly elected to the presidency; and Cotton Mather's hopes definitely ended.

III

Despite his conviction that Harvard was going to the dogs — a conviction of which his father had been sure many years earlier — Cotton Mather had reason to believe that orthodox Christian education might still be safe in New England. In 1701 a college in Connecticut was established by ten clergymen, graduates of Harvard. In 1702 teaching began, but students were scattered in various towns under various tutors. In 1717 the college was established at New Haven; and in the next year its first building was completed. Cotton Mather had been interested in the college from the start. He had been among those consulted about a scheme for a " collegiate school " in 1701; he had sent it books; he had proposed " an hopeful Gentleman " to its presidency when that office was vacant; and he had watched its progress with the more hope as Harvard became more liberal. When in

1718 the college had been formally established at New Haven and the first building was nearing completion, Cotton Mather conceived the idea of writing for help for the college " unto a wealthy East-India merchant at London, who may be disposed on several accounts to do for that Society and Colony." On his own initiative he wrote to Elihu Yale: " The Colony of Connecticut, having for some years had a College at Saybrook without a collegious way of living for it, have lately begun to erect a large edifice for it in the town of New Haven. The charge of that expensive building is not yet all paid, nor are there yet any funds of revenues for salaries to the Professors and Instructors to the Society.

" Sir, though you have your felicities in your family, which I pray God continue and multiply, yet certainly, if what is forming at New Haven might wear the name of YALE COLLEGE, it would be better than *a name of sons and daughters*. And your munificence might easily obtain for you such a commemoration and perpetuation of your valuable name, which would indeed be much better than an Egyptian pyramid."

Seven months later Cotton Mather wrote to Governor Saltonstall confessing *" that it was a great and inexcusable presumption in me, to make myself so far the godfather of the beloved infant as to propose a name* for it. But I assured myself, that if a succession of solid and lasting benefits might be entailed upon it your Honor and the Honorable Trustees would pardon me, and the proposal would be complied withal."

That Mather had hopes that Yale would reach a state

of religious grace denied to Harvard is plain enough, as
he continues: " When the servants of God meet at your
Commencement, I make no doubt, that, under your
Honor's influences and encouragements, they will make
it an opportunity, in the moſt serious and mature manner,
to deliberate upon projeċtions to serve the great intereſts
of education, and so of religion, both in your College and
throughout your Colony, as well as whatever else may
advance the kingdom of God, and not suffer an interview
of your beſt men to evaporate such a senseless, useless,
noisy impertinency, as it uses to do with us at Cambridge."

At all events, in the same year Elihu Yale sent to
Boſton for the college at New Haven three bales of as-
sorted merchandise which sold for five hundred and
sixty-two pounds twelve shillings ſterling, and the success of the new college was assured. Nor did Cotton
Mather ever relinquish his intereſt in Yale. When its
reċtor in 1722 turned to the Church of England, Mather
was offered his place; he wrote to Governor Saltonſtall
about his son's visit to Connecticut in 1724, and Yale
conferred the maſter's degree upon this boy " yett short
of eighteen years of age." In some measure, then, the
success of Yale offset the disappointment of Harvard. At
leaſt New England had an orthodox school to provide,
as he had written to Elihu Yale, " The supply of all their
synagogues."

IV

Though to the colleges Cotton Mather was thoroughly
conservative, he was not conservative enough for the

[223]

leaders of thought in Massachusetts. When Cotton Mather and two other Boston ministers signed, with representatives of five ministerial associations, the *Proposals of 1705* urging a " consociation of churches " to bring the independent churches of Massachusetts into a union whereby each church would lose some of its independence for the sake of the federation, they were regarded by men of the old school as dangerous innovators. Most articulate and most virulent of the ultra-conservatives was John Wise of Ipswich, who earlier in 1687 had dared, with a group of his neighbours, to defy Sir Edmund Andros, the first royal governor. For his defiance he stood trial, was told by Joseph Dudley that he and his friends had " no more privileges left [them] than not to be sold for Slaves," was fined heavily, and was suspended " from the Ministerial Function." He had served as chaplain with Phips against Quebec, and in 1692 had dared to join thirty-two others in a written appeal for John Proctor, after Proctor's condemnation for witchcraft. A shrewd, independent, homespun man of the people, he saw in the *Proposals of 1705* a movement away from the good old independent way of the seventeenth-century churches. He rose in his honest wrath and in *The Churches Quarrel Espoused* issued in 1710 and reprinted in Boston in 1715, and in *A Vindication of the Government of New England Churches* printed in Boston in 1717, put an end to the proposal of a federal union of churches by a passionate appeal to the ingrained prejudices of New England country-folk. Apparently he lost no opportunity of landing a blow, for in helping the establishment of a church in 1714 " Mr. Wise [gave] the Right Hand of Fellow-ship, much applauding the N. English venerable Consti-tution." New England was well launched upon its habit of foreshortening antiquity. To Cotton Mather, Wise was a " furious man " and his book a " foolish, cursed Libel."

In 1715 at a fast at the Brattle Church, Cotton Mather preached against Wise, " Excellently: censur'd him that had reproach'd the Ministry, calling the Proposals Mo-dalities of little consequence . . . call'd it a Satanick insult, twice over, and it found a kind Reception. . . . " But in the end the rough Yankee preacher won, and years later at the Revolution the voice of his village democracy spoke from his grave to support the " natural rights " of the " embattled farmers."

The most violent of Cotton Mather's public conflicts was the one which, in the mind of the modern world, did him most honor, the conflict over inoculation for smallpox.

v

In the spring of 1721 there came to Boston a violent epidemic of smallpox. Nearly half of the inhabitants con-tracted it before it wore itself out, and one in fourteen died. Its coming caused Cotton Mather no little anxiety. In the first place, he had predicted " the speedy Ap-proach of the destroying Angel "; now it was here the vanity of his successful forecast would surely bring upon him the wrath of God. Then he had two children who were not immune. Finally he displayed the calm heroism of the seasoned pastor who in that day brought more comfort than the physician. " My own Life is likely to be extremely in danger, by the horrid Venom of the sick Chambers, which I muſt look to be call'd unto; and I would accordingly Redeem the Time to do what my hand finds to do."

He was sure that he could confer one benefit upon Boſton — he had never forgotten his medical intereſt — by spreading the news of inoculation, a treatment he had learned from a publication of the Royal Society lent him by Dr. William Douglass, the only physician in Boſton with a medical degree and the one moſt inhospitable to the new idea. This was not vaccination in the modern method, but inoculation which induced a mild form of the disease. Though it had never been tried in America, Mather felt sure that many lives could be saved by it. Therefore he prepared a ſtatement for the Boſton physicians embodying a summary of the Royal Society publications. Dr. Douglass fell into a rage, recalled the publication he had lent Mather, and refused to lend it to anyone. A bitter enemy of inoculation, he transferred some of his enmity to the miniſter who had ventured into a physician's territory. Dr. Zabdiel Boylſton, however, became intereſted, made inquiries among the Boſton negroes who had used inoculation, and thereafter became the leading advocate of the praćtice, inoculating his own children.

Immediately there rose a " horrid Clamour " againſt Mather and Boylſton. Since people knew nothing of the medicall merits of the queſtion they brought the charge that it was a heathen praćtice used by negroes and Turks, and that a Chriſtian could not lawfully learn from the heathen. A war of pamphlets and of newspaper articles raged, with Cotton Mather believing himself the center of abuse in the " monstrous and crying Wickedness " of Boston. His son Samuel requested inoculation. While he was ill his father was in a whirl of doubt. What if the boy should die? " besides the Loss of so hopeful a Son, I should also suffer a prodigious Clamour and Hatred from an infuriated Mob, whom the Devil has inspired with a most hellish Rage. . . . The Town is become almost a Hell upon Earth, a City full of Lies, and Murders, and Blasphemies. . . . Satan seems to take a strange Possession of it, in the epidemic Rage, against that notable and powerful and successful way of saving the Lives of People from the Dangers of *Small-pox.*"

Meanwhile Samuel recovered. But Hannah, her father's " poor Nancy, dear Nancy," was very ill; and Abigail died in childbirth.

With these troubles at home it was the more distressing to face new calumnies from his enemies. Allied with the narrow-minded Dr. Douglass was John Checkley, a witty young man, educated abroad, the keeper of a shop that combined an apothecary's, a bookshop, and a variety store. Checkley was ready to join any journalistic fight, especially one against the clergy singly or as a whole. Checkley it was who first thought of harassing Mather on the question of his membership in the Royal Society. Mather had never visited England and hence had never gone through the ceremony of investiture which would have completed the formality of admission. The rules of the society at this time did not permit the inclusion in the printed lists of members the names of any one who

[227]

had not been so invested. Consequently, neither Mather's name nor Brattle's was in the list. In the malicious attacks which followed, Brattle's title was not once questioned — in fact he did not, apparently, figure in this fight against Mather. Dr. Douglass with the meanness of a small mind immediately seized upon this new weapon, declaring in a published tract that doubtless the Royal Society had repudiated Cotton Mather, and intimating that the University of Glasgow might follow suit and recall his D.D. He maliciously paraphrased Mather's discussion of inoculation, and in writing to England took it upon himself to apologize for Mather's communication as credulous and vain. Checkley went further, writing to the secretary of the Royal Society a direct query as to Mather's membership, asking the answer to be addressed to himself as " Dr. John Checkley," the title of doctor proper only to doctors of divinity having by this time been appropriated by " pothecarys & midwives." Neither Checkley nor Douglass was aware that Dr. James Jurin, the new secretary of the society, was a most ardent advocate of inoculation who in his own address to the society had quoted Cotton Mather as an authority.

Meantime Mather himself wrote for either affirmation or repudiation of his title. Checkley was in London when the Royal Society made its answer to Mather and to the world. In an unusually large meeting the secretary, to dissolve all doubts due to a former secretary's carelessness and the enmity of Boston men, put Mather's name to the vote, receiving unanimous confirmation of his election. As the clause had not yet been inserted permitting omission of the formal inauguration, Mather's name was never printed in the lift of members. But now it did not matter that the lift viciously pofted in Hall's Coffee House in Bofton by Douglass or Checkley did not contain his name; it did not matter what lies were told by Bofton's "Hell Fire Club," that "Society of Physicians Anti-Inoculators" headed by Checkley. Mather was officially declared an F.R.S.; and furthermore, the society had nothing but praise and admiration for his fight againft smallpox.

Nevertheless, he could not gain many adherents to his belief in inoculation. The opposition increased until one night, "as it grew towards Morning . . ., some unknown Hands, threw a fired Granado into the Chamber where my Kinsman lay, and which uses to be my Lodging-Room. The Weight of the Iron Ball alone, had it fallen upon his Head, would have been enough to have done part of the Business designed." But the fuse broke off since "*this Night there ftood by me the Angel of the* GOD, *whose I am and whom I serve,*" and so no mischief was done except to bestow upon Mather almoft a martyr's crown. To the "granado" was tied a paper expressing in the vigorous language of the Puritans the sender's feelings: "COTTON MATHER, You Dog, Dam you: I'll inoculate you with this, with a Pox to you." The miraculously preserved Mather in an account written for the *Bofton News-Letter* gave the inscription with this addition: "Cotton Mather, I was once one of your Meeting, but the cursed Lie you told of ———, you know who, made me leave you, you Dog; . . ." Now Mather's mind was irradiated with the holy joy of approaching martyrdom; the " granado " would, he felt sure, be followed by other attacks, and soon he would be even as the martyrs who " testified formerly in the Flames of *Smithfield.*" But as the dreaded disease burned itself out, inoculation ceased to be a main point of discussion, and the fickle fury of the Boston mob found other folk to rend.

Open fight brought exhilaration to Cotton Mather; to take up arms for the Lord was a joyous exercise; to confound His enemies a bright privilege. There were some troubles, however, against which one could not fight; they could be met only with resignation. Such was the deep disappointment over the *Biblia Americana.* In 1693 he had set himself " every Morning to write upon a Portion of *Scripture,* some *Illustration,* that should have in it, something of Curiositie." In the *Magnalia,* which he finished in 1697, he promised that if the Lord spared his life he would " make unto the Church of God an humble tender of our *Biblia Americana,* a volume enriched with better things than all the plate of the Indies; *yet not I but the* GRACE OF CHRIST WITH ME." In 1706 his " Amassment of *Illustrations,* with which, I hope one day to send out our *Biblia Americana* " has reached " very many Thousands." This year it was finished; " 'Twil be two large Volumes in *Folio;* and I am now to wait upon the Lord, for His Direction, how to obtain a conveyance of the Manuscripts, into those Hands, that may publish them for the Service of His Churches." But in spite of the Lord's " wonderful Smiles on [the] Undertaking," he had long to wait. Though he prayed, and published advertisements, and hoped for the aid of " eminent and opulent Persons," and wrote to England, and added a thousand illuſtrations in a single year, and made *" A New Offer, to the Lovers of Religion and Learning,"* yet " Strange Frowns of Heaven " were upon him. In 1716 " with the sweeteſt Acquiescence and Resignation " he received " Advice . . . that the publication [of the *Biblia Americana*] is to be despaired of." He had need of resignation, for the great work in six folio volumes ſtill remains in manuscript, a dinosaur of biblical ſtudy.

VI

Like his public life, Cotton Mather's family life in his laſt years brought him only anxiety and grief.

Only a month after the death of his second wife in 1713 he was finding it necessary to fight againſt " any Idea of those grateful Circumſtances which I have heretofore enjoy'd in the married State." " Silly People " urged him to marry again; " a foolish Message from a Gentlewoman " was brought to him. Almoſt weekly he prayed againſt impurity; regularly, cases of men fallen into " vicious Courses " perturbed him.

In 1714 John George, probably the same " facetious George " who in 1710 had brought Mather his degree of D.D. from Glasgow, died. His widow was Lydia, daughter of a physician and miniſter who, having lived for a time in Massachusetts, had on a journey abroad been taken captive by the French, in which condition he died, thereby earning a biography in Mather's *Magnalia*. Lydia George was apparently a rather gay, flirtatious creature, for early in 1701 she consulted her pastor, the attractive young Benjamin Colman, about the wisdom of her rich and fashionable apparel. How real her scruples were or how real her desire to attract the attention of her spiritual adviser, can but be imagined. The answer of Colman must have gratified her at the time; and must in later years have given her a weapon to use against Cotton Mather when his scruples against things of the flesh were most obnoxious to her. Mr. Colman wrote a very long letter indeed, going into the matter of attire and scruples fully, among other things saying: " Now for my own part I freely profess, I think your dress is suitable to your age, Estate, & the sober fashion of your degree, birth & Education. Why you should think of changing your apparel I should see no reason, & that what you wear should discompose you for God's worship is to me unaccountable. . . .

" I have this to add over & above, You have been educated in the wearing rich apparel; Mr. George chuses you should continue it, it is not offensive or grievous to sober Christians: It is not good to indulge scruples too much, for they will grow upon you apace to your great discomfort: & you are to fear lest this or any suchlike scruples prove but a temptation to take conscience off in judging us for some greater matter."

Less than two months after Lydia George's husband's death the neighbours were talking, and her pastor, Mr. Colman, had apparently seen fit to remonstrate with Cotton Mather about his visits to the lady. On the third of January, 1715, Mather wrote to Colman, " . . . the neighbours will no more have the Leaſt occasion given them, to suspeƈt me of any Designs not proper for me. . . . My heart would Reproach me, if I had not more than one hundred Thoughts of my Death, to one of the Fancy my Neighbours talk of." Nevertheless, death did not approach and the lady received a flattering though dignified letter which seemed to suggeſt serious courtship. It was not, however, a definite proposal; and the lady coyly responded that she was sure he could find " other persons more agreeable "; that she muſt forbid his writing to her; that if he weren't a minſter she couldn't allow him even to call upon her; and anyhow he muſt not talk of marriage — a word not yet uttered by him. His next move was to tumble squarely into her net. He wrote to a friend, aƈting apparently as intermediary, that since she thought it too soon after her husband's death to receive attentions, he would acquiesce in her decision in order to ſtop gossip; but he would not therefore " lay aside " hopes or promise not to renew his advances.

Mrs. George did not long prove obdurate; she soon accepted from him a thorough-going love letter that urged her to love God firſt, but then His image in Cotton Mather:

" My —— (Inexpressible!) I am afraid you been't well, because my Head has aked pretty much this Afternoon.

" The pain of my Heart, will be much greater than that of my Head, if it be really so.

" But I imagine, you are growing well, because my Headake is going off.

" Your Little Daughter [Mather had young children at this time; Mrs. George's one daughter was already married] waits upon you, to bring me the agreeable satisfaction.

" May you to-morrow, (and praeparatory to it,) have sweet Interviews, with Him, whom your soul Loveth!

" What is He, more than any other Beloved! O infinitely more! All others, pretenders in your esteem and I among the rest, are black and base and vile things, yea, and the brightest Angels in Heaven, are mean Things in Comparison of Him. O Sun in the Firmament; Thou art all Blackness, before that sun of Righteousness.

" Think so, my dear, grow in such Thoughts; and Lose the sight of all things but Him.

" I mightily wish, That you may Love nothing that is Mine. My wishes are, That I may be so Happy as to exhibit unto you some Reflections of His Image. If you can discover anything of [*illegible*] in the meanest of men, 'tis well. Every thing else, Dislike it. And the more you will be Lik'd and Lov'd by

" One who Loves you Inexpressibly (and . . . most affectionately and compassionately."

Perhaps this undated letter was written the day before his marriage, which came in July, when he and Lydia George were united, and he could write to their intermediary, " I am now *There*."

Lydia George was quite different from her predecessors. Rather did she resemble that lovely damsel whom Mather had been obliged to relinquish for the glory of God. She was well educated; she was bright and witty in her conversation; she was fond of worldly things; and had her birth, her station, and her reputation not been irreproachable, she would, in all her allure of physical charms, have seemed an instrument of Satan. But all her credentials were unquestionable; and her husband could rejoice in his good fortune and revel in his happiness. His wife was " The best of women in the American World," a " rich Blessing," the greatest of all his " Temporal Blessings "; as a consort she was " valuable," " dear," and " lovelie." She was " an excellent Mother " for his children. Eight months later he again thanked God for this quality in her, adding in the margin years later: " Ah! quam deceptus! " (Alas! how I was deceived!)

But at first all was contentment in his household. Life was a perpetual honeymoon for this man of fifty-two. The sickness of his daughters did not break the rhythm of his happiness, though it did lead him to lament his lost habit of holding fast days and make him attempt to renew the custom. In August, 1716, more than a year after marriage, he wrote: " I am afraid, lest the Multiplicity of my Affaires, and my easy Circumstances, procure some Abatement of those Ejaculations towards Heaven, with an Eye continually unto the Lord, which I am used unto. Oh! it must not be so! It must not be so! " Like many another uxorious man, he relaxed to enjoy life with his wife. He rode abroad with a company of gentlemen and ladies " to take the countrey Air, and to divert ourselves, at a famous Fish-pond! " Mather unfortunately tumbled out of the canoe and might have drowned but that they were near the shore. He earnestly considered whether he was " quickly to go under the Earth, as I have been under the Water," and his consort's mind was troubled for his safety.

" A Drowsiness, upon the Activity " of his living to God seemed to grow upon him. But various happenings soon made him throw himself once more on the mercy of God with continued prayers and fasts; with the feeling that " a praying Life " must be " more than ever encouraged and animated " with him. He had already noted that his wife had a specially pious soul. With him she prayed earnestly for her daughter who had married in 1708 " an Husband, who has proved one of the worst of Men; a sorry, sordid, froward and exceedingly wicked Fellow. His Life would have kill'd the Child; and have utterly confounded, not only her temporal Interest, but my Wife's also. . . . almost a year ago, I began to have some Irradiations on my Mind, . . . that before a Year came about, they should see a deliverance. However, I could not bring about my Purposes, to beseach the Lord thrice, until towards the Beginning of the Winter. But then, I kept *three dayes of Prayer,* in every one of which, a principal Errand unto Heaven was, to putt over this wicked Creature into the Hands of the holy God, that in His Way, and in His Time, the poor Child might be delivered from his insupportable Tyrannies; but above all, that it might be by his becoming a new Creature, if that might be obtained." But apparently that was asking too much even of Omnipotence, for no sooner had the third day of prayer been held " but God smote the Wretch, with a languishing Sickness, which no body ever knew what to

[236]

make of. He was a ſtrong, lively, hearty young Man; a little above thirty; But now, he languished for *six Months;* nor were any of our Physicians, tho' he successively employ'd no less than five of them, able to help him. In this while, our Faith, our Love, our Patience, and our Submission to the Will of God, underwent many Trials more precious than Gold. But on the laſt *Wednesday,* the glorious GOD putt a Period unto the *grievous Wayes* of this wicked Man." But his sons remained to cause Cotton Mather trouble until they drowned while skating on Boſton Common only a short time before the end of Mather's own life. For Mather, with no experience of business, undertook the adminiſtration of the eſtate in behalf of Mrs. Howell, his ſtepdaughter, and her two sons. Seven months later Mrs. Howell married Samuel Sewall, the nephew of the famous Judge, Mather's close friend. From the ſtart Mather's business inexperience was againſt him; and the adminiſtration of the eſtate brought vexation and worry. Four years later, in 1720, he drew up a brief, urging that he be freed from this burden for " the sufferings of the present Adminiſtrator are . . . insupportable." At the same time Judge Sewall received an anonymous letter in Cotton Mather's behalf. This letter blamed Sewall's nephew for " his barbarous carriage " toward Mather. " His Tirrible wife," the letter proceeded, " . . . will have a great *Eſtate* whether there be one or no. the women talk like mad people about it. . . . Good Sir make haſte with your helping hand to this diſtressed afflicted miniſter of Chriſt and save him from the Plotts of those whom you may see would ruin him." Mather may, in desperation, have written this letter; he may have written it and given it to a friend to copy and send; a disinterested person may have written it — at all events it proves him in serious straits.

In 1721 the administration was still unfinished. " And my Children-in-Law, have laid a deep Design, assisted with crafty and cruel Adversaries, if they can, to ruine me." He was now in " considerable *Poverty,*" his possessions were sold, he no longer owned a " Foot of Land in all the World." His salary was too small, he was restricted in the usual abundance and quality of his food and clothes. In 1724, after seven years of worry, he wrote: " I have Arrests laid upon me, for considerable Sums; whereof really I owe not a Farthing. And I have no Prospects of any Out-gate, but by selling all my Goods to pay the Debts. . . . O thou strong Redeemer; I sink, I sink; Oh! Reach out thy Hand and save me! " At last, when all seemed over, some of his parishioners raised " a Summ of considerably more than two hundred Pounds, to pay a Debt of my wife's former Husband, which I inconsiderately had made my own." For his thanks he published a " Discourse on the *Unsearchable Riches of CHRIST* and with an agreeable Dedication of it unto the Flock." He was the more impelled to give them public thanks since he had privately confided to his diary a few weeks earlier: " My Friends have . . . a deep Sleep from the Lord fallen upon them: and tho' they might easily putt a stop to my Confusions, they, like Persons in a Maze and a doze, permitt them to go on, unto such Extremity, that within a Fortnight I must

[238]

either be lodg'd in the Prison, or forc'd into a private Withdraw, which where and how it will terminate, none can foresee." But neither his person nor his library was seized; his parishioners came to the rescue, and three years later the troublesome boys fell through the ice and ceased from troubling.

VII

But Mather's own son during these years had been a source of much greater woe. This was that younger Increase, his dearly loved Cresy, whose birth seemed to be under such auspicious omens. For Cotton Mather on a Saturday night, feeling that he muſt keep fit for his Sunday's labors, went to sleep about midnight, having commended his consort (the firſt wife) unto the Lord. An hour later, however, he awoke perturbed, and arose, going not to his wife, but to his ſtudy, where on his knees he expressed himself unworthy of mercy, imploring His Mercy to his " Consort, in the Diſtress now upon her. While my Faith was pleading, that the Saviour who was *born of a Woman,* would send His good Angel to releeve my Consort, the People ran to my ſtudy-door with Tidings, *that a Son was born unto mee.* I continued then on my Knees, praising the Lord; and I received a wonderful Advice from Heaven, that this my Son, shall bee a Servant of my Lord Jesus Chriſt throughout eternal Ages.

" Hee was born, about three Quarters of an Hour paſt one, in the morning, of the Lord's-day . . . an hearty, luſty and comely Infant.

" In the Afternoon, I baptised my Son, and in Honour

to my Parent, I called him, INCREASE. After which, retiring to my Study, it was again assured mee from Heaven, that this Child shall glorify my Lord Jesus Christ, and bee with Him, to behold His Glory."

It is curious to note that the birth of the second son, who also lived to grow up, was not accompanied by any such assurances. His father merely noted his " desire to have him devoted unto the Service of the Lord, as long as he lives." This son Samuel, born seven years after Cresy, became a competent, moderately successful clergyman, the fourth in direct line from Richard Mather, and the only dull one. Throughout his childhood his father's chief concern for him was " Sammy's inordinate love of play."

Cresy, whose birth started auspiciously, went through twenty-five riotous years, following the path, not of his saintly fathers, but of the two wicked brothers of his mother, with perhaps a throw-back to his great-uncle John Cotton, whose " Notorious Breaches of the Seventh Commandment " had banished him two years before Cresy's birth. The career of this younger Increase was full of joy for him and of woe for his father. Quite young he attached himself to the wrong sort of companion in spite of his careful training — he had been taught by his grandfather and then sent to school where his father hoped he would use his exercises in writing themes for godly discourse. His father spent much time and thought over the education of all his children. He gave up to them special hours for exhortation and prayer; he set them exercises which should combine learning and piety; he

[240]

had them translate his own pious writings into Latin. He tried never to come into their company, even by chance, even and especially when they were at play, without letting fall some noteworthy remarks that should be a source of improvement to them. As a servant of God he felt it incumbent upon him always to work for the improvement of others, and to make the words of his mouth, especially to his wife and children, contain exemplary material. But he also carried in his pocket sweetmeats which he beſtowed upon all children he met.

He was far ahead of the times in the matters both of education and of discipline. He objeĉted to the prevailing mode of beating knowledge into the young; his children were brought up to regard inſtruĉtion as a favor, the denial of it a punishment. Even Cresy cried when his grandfather, because he dallied on the way, refused one morning to teach him; and his father interceded for him. At table Mather would entertain his children with lively ſtories, not always from the Bible. Perhaps he originated this scheme of sugar-coated inſtruĉtion which seems to us entirely modern. He made it a point to get home by nine o'clock at night in order to give his children an hour before their bedtime. He was pleased when some of his children desired to learn French. He saw to it that his daughters as well as his sons were really educated. Latin and even Hebrew might well be taught them; and all his children were to learn shorthand. One daughter he seleĉted to learn medicine, as a useful and intereſting field of knowledge for a woman. Busy as he was, he tried always to supervise his children's education, their manners, and their religion; all in a way calculated not to repress but to stimulate their desire to improve.

Cresy, however, did not respond; he played with gunpowder and got scorched; he wasted his time with riotous youngsters; he was neither physically nor mentally sober. His father was confident that with manhood his foolishness would leave him. In time he came to see that Cresy would never make a minister, and he looked about to settle him in secular business, always hoping to find a godly master for him. The lad went to England where, suffering with rheumatism, he stayed with his uncle Samuel who rather resented having to be responsible for such a nephew and at the same time to act as placing agent for Cotton Mather's white elephant, the *Biblia Americana*. He prudently kept Cresy from the lure of London, writing to Cresy's father: " Your son is with me I must keep a pretty strict eye over him for if left to himself he will not escape sinne in a place of Temptation. He told me his grandfather was coming over and that you intended to send him a remittance by him which made me the more willingly invite him to stay with me till the next spring. His Grandfather's not coming makes his affairs to be in a puzled state. He came with but ten shillings in his pocket to Witney. . . . He had but one shirt and was so bare in every respect that I was perfectly ashamed. I take care to let him have credit with our Countrey Shopkeepers at Witney that he may have Linnen and Woollen suitable and handsome. I propose that you make a genteel remittance to Him, but let the Money come into Mr. Sodens hands to manage it for him.

I perceive he is infected with the disease which is the blemish of the Family viz. to spend inconsiderately and take no thought about providing against future unavoidable occasions. If I can I will cure him. I design to keep him at Witney 'till just the Instant of his going off to N. England again left the Snares of London should occasion his returning to His Father with a worse character then he had when he came. . . ."

This young man about whom his father had once written: " How marvellously does the glorious Lord glorify me, in that which is the First-born of my Desires! " and about whom he had written many times, " My poor Son Increase! " returned to meet his second Stepmother " much polished, much improved, better than ever disposed; with Articles of less Expense to me than I expected; and, which is wonderful, with an excellent Business prepared for him immediately to fall into." His father was " astonished at the Favours of the prayer-hearing Lord " and more than ever hoped to " fix the returned Child for the Service of God! "

Within a year and a half, however, Cresy added to his list of minor misbehaviors by public scandal. ". . . an Harlot big with a Bastard, accuses my poor son *Cresy,* and layes her Belly to him. Oh! . . . Sorrow beyond any that I have mett withal! " wrote his grieved and yet sympathetic father. It helped somewhat to have the " most sensible Judges " believe the boy innocent, but the humiliation was very great. Perhaps Cotton Mather's greatest grief was the fear that he ought to repudiate this dearly loved son. He kept the boy confined at home until the storm of gossip should " be blown over," and his wife joined him in prayer for the lad. Cotton Mather felt that perhaps all this scandal was but " a dreadful Way " for Cresy's conversion. In a day of fast and prayer he felt that in promising to give his son up if he did not reform he had done his utmost; he was not even sure that he could make such a sacrifice unless God would help him " in the sacrificing Stroke, to go as far as any of His children commonly go in the present State of Mortality."

Not quite two weeks later Cresy got into some new scrape and his father was convinced that his prayers were not heard; yet he felt that there might still be " unknown Reserves of Mercy." Cresy obviously tapped them all, for the next summer the diary of his father was full of " New Distresses " about his " poor son *Increase!* " and from time to time, alas! only too frequently, occur the pathetic entries: " My GOD! My GOD! " and " O my GOD, my SAVIOUR; From the Depths I cry unto thee."

Five years after he had returned from England much improved, Cresy had become " my wicked Son *Increase* " to whom it was necessary to write " a tremendous Letter " offering a choice between repentance and disinheritance. And in sadness Cotton Mather wrote, " Lord, tho' I am a *Dog,* yett cast out the Devil, that has possession of the Child."

Now his father had to admit him to be " ungodly, distracted, hard-hearted," abandoned to " foolish and vicious Courses, which must bring him to Misery," and his father " into unspeakable Trouble and Anguish and Confusion." But his devoted parent could not wholly relinquish him, nor could he even for a little forget him: " Ah, Poor *Increase,* Tho' I spake againſt him, yett I earneſtly remember him, and my Bowels are troubled for him. Is there nothing further to be done? His Grandfather, and his Kinsmen and others, muſt labour with him."

After a few months Mather, like many another forgiving and fond father, invited his son to return home, rationalizing his desire to have the boy with him by saying that thus he might have him continually under his eye.

Increase finally went to sea and disappeared forever with his ship. At this time — 1724 — Mather was having more than the usual troubles with his wife; and though his son Samuel was turning out all that was moſt creditable and gratifying, his heart was wrung for this beloved black sheep. He could but hope that Increase's laſt letters were sincere and heartfelt, for then his father could feel hopeful of his salvation. Two weeks later came a rumor that the boat had not been loſt, but had reached Newfoundland. Cotton Mather's joy was great; the news, however, proved false and he could but say, *" Lord, Thou haſt lifted me up, and caſt me down,* Oh! " Cresy was gone.

Only a year before had died the prop of Cotton Mather's life, his father. Cotton had been " Mr. Mather the younger " until he was paſt sixty; and in the less than five years of life left him he scarcely ſtepped out of the shadow of his father. Death seems to have called a halt to temporal quarrels and men who reviled the living were

often bearers at their laſt rites. So " Mr. President Leverett " helped to bear what was left of his ſtout adversary
to his final reſting-place " by his firſt wife."

There was never the slighteſt doubt in Cotton Mather's
mind but that a death commanded a publication. For
his wives and children the funeral sermon was fitting
enough tribute; for his father, the greateſt influence of
his life, something more was called for. And in time he
could communicate to a correspondent: " I have Lately
written, *Memoirs of Remarkable Things in the Life and
the Death* of my deceased Parent. But, it being a Book
of it may be Twenty Sheets, it will be diverse Months
before our otherwise employ'd presses can give it to the
public. In the mean time, I transmit unto you, a *Coe-
leſtinus* that will bring something of and from the
Countrey which he is gone unto."

A younger and a less patient man might have signal-
ized his freedom by a series of independent actions such
as his father would have frowned upon. Moſt of us, being
human, are apt to celebrate our firſt hours of unsupervised activity by greater or lesser foolishness. But Cotton
Mather was paſt sixty; he had been trained in the way
his father wished him to go since he could firſt speak or
underſtand; and the few remaining years of his life he
continued under the harness his father had fashioned
for him, none the less guided because the hands that held
the reins were ſtill.

VIII

If in his second widowhood Mather had found " a
Sacrificing Life, to be fuller of ſtrong and ſtrange Conso-

lations, than can be imagined by one, who has made no Trial of it," his later years, what with troubles over his son, his stepdaughter's children, and his temperamental wife, offered him plenty of opportunity for testing his theory. If he in his courtship with Lydia George suffered so much in spirit and health that he was " unhinged " for his employments, in his marriage he was much further hindered. At first it was his complete satisfaction that made difficulty for him; later it was what a less dignified age would call incompatibility of temper. For Lydia George when she became Lydia Mather did not lay aside her worldly frivolities. She expected her husband to remain her lover. By the time Cotton Mather was fifty-five he began to rationalize his declining desire by finding that the Lord demanded from him the sacrifice of " Enjoyment." He still felt, however, that he and his family all possessed a rich blessing in his consort.

But he soon noted in his diary, writing this time in Greek characters that his wife might not be able to understand: " The Diseases of my soul are not cured until I arrive to the most unspotted Chastitie and Puritie.

" I do not apprehend that Heaven requires me to utterlie lay aside my fondness for my lovelie Consort."

And then in English: " But I must mourn most bitterlie and walk humblie all my Daies for my former pollutions. I must abhor the least tho't of regard unto anie other Person but this dearlie beloved of my soul. I must be temperate in my Conversation with her. And I must alwaies propose a good and an high End in it; something that mai be an expression or an Evidence of my Obedience to God."

Lydia George was already a grandmother when she married Mather; and this marriage was childless. Hence his scruples, which were probably the greater in that this wife herself had no scruples. She was obviously a highly sexed woman who had no regard for an abstemious husband. She treated Mather with " a Fondness, that it may be, few Wives in the World have arrived at." When she was ill he determined that he must always be pious in her presence and never be with her without speaking something worth her considering and remembering. He tended to sink the husband in the priest, an end she neither foresaw nor welcomed. Her " Grievous Outbreakings of her proud passions " led him in less than four years after marriage to record: " The Consort, in whom I flattered myself with the View and Hopes of an uncommon Enjoyment, has dismally confirmed it unto me, that our *Idols* must prove our *Sorrows*."

In the year that had just passed he felt that he had made " more Advances in Piety, than in many former Years " and had kept many days of prayer. But his wife was not interested in an increase of piety. She saw her husband slipping away from her; and her rage at losing him to God was as great as — or perhaps greater than — it would have been had his attentions been diverted by another woman. In that case she could have found some satisfaction in blaming and reviling the other woman; she

[248]

could hardly reproach God. She did her beſt by making a mess of his papers, deſtroying some, hiding others. Cotton Mather began to think that death would be sweet. He was not above taking revenge upon his wife, however, by writing more than ever; her attempts to ſtop his pious labors would merely augment his " Fruitfulness."

Any attempt to assuage her jealousy by devoting a little more time to her simply did not occur to him. He went painfully about his own way, not yielding in the leaſt. When her jealousy extended to his favorite daughter, he removed that daughter from the house.

In 1724 he noted in Latin that his home was in every way peaceful with his wife ecſtatically in love with him; two weeks later the " insanity " of his wife had once more plunged the family into misery. A few days later tranquillity was reſtored; and this time he was at ease, for his wife expressed for him not the usual moſt passionate (*flagrantissimum*) love, but the deepeſt admiration. He now hoped to overcome her malignant spirit and lead her in the proper path animated not alone by love of her husband, but by fear of God.

Now there was some danger of his being once more fonder than his growing asceticism approved: " O! Lett my Conversation with my Consort be full of all Goodness, and more than ever exhibit in it a Conformity to the good One, and a Pattern to all Observers!

" But then, O! Lett all possible Purity accompany it, and lett me watch againſt all such inordinate Affeƈtion, as may grieve the holy Spirit of GOD! " He felt that he ought to be useful to his consort and share with her his holy thoughts, especially those with which he fell asleep.

Holy thoughts were not, however, to his wife's liking; and after the most flagrant (*flagrantissimos*) exhibitions of love she fell into a great rage — doubtless over his failure to respond. Passion in women was not proper; a passionate wife was surely mad. There was no other way to explain her fits of fury alternating with fits of ardent love. Her " enamoured Fondness " led her to reproach him with a lack of kindness. He either failed or chose not to understand. She said his "Looks and Words were not so very kind as they had been. A mere Fancy and Whimsey! But the bare telling her so, threw her into these Violences, wherein she charged me with Crimes, which obliged me to rebuke her lying Tongue, with Terms I have not been used unto." The sedate minister had obviously been stung into most undignified recriminations. He left her raving, and retired to his study to pray; whereupon the indignant lady woke " her wicked Niece and Maid," whom Mather had previously designated as a wicked and malicious " lyar," and the two of them, though it was past midnight, sought refuge in a neighbour's house.

Mather's son and daughter arose and joined him in lengthy prayer after which he went to bed and " enjoy'd some Repose." He tried to gather what comfort he could out of his forced celibacy: " . . . my Consort's leaving of my Bed, when I am a Person of whom there cannot be the least Pretence of my being a Person universally acceptable, affords me Occasion of particular Supplica-

tions, that the Holiness and Purity whereto I am so
singularly called of GOD, may have its perfect work, and
that I may no longer foolishly dote as I have done, upon
a Person who treats me with such a matchless Ingratitude,
and Malignity."

However, his wife speedily returned, begging that all
might be forgotten and that he would pray with her for
their future harmony. He " did accordingly. And the
Tokens of the greatest Inamoration on her part ensued
upon it." If the only way to reach this husband of hers
was through piety, then Lydia Mather would become
pious. With all serene, Cotton Mather resolved, to preserve the tranquillity of his household, to pray oftener
with his consort, adding besides this, one more prayer to
his daily set of six. For months now " by a marvellous
Operation of the divine Providence " all things ran
smoothly in his family, his great grief over Cresy's death
softening as time went on. In preparing for the press
the sermon he preached on his son's death he felt that " the
Child, who did so little Good, but much ill, in all the
Days of his Life," might thus " do some good at his
Death."

But as Mather grew increasingly pious, becoming more
and more absorbed in an attempt to make his life conform
with Christ's, the sympathy between him and his wife
necessarily lessened. He preferred to call her mad,
honestly believing her so. He was relieved when the public acquaintance of her madness — her flight during the
night could hardly be concealed — did not harm him in
his ministry. She could hardly state her case in a way to

arouse sympathy for herself in a Puritan community. And she lived to mourn him and be called his disconsolate widow in Samuel Mather's uninspired biography of his father.

IX

It was in December, 1727, that Cotton Mather's laſt illness finally settled down upon him, perhaps haſtened by especially ſtrenuous activities over the earthquake in October. Such a direct speaking of God muſt have a meaning; and the miniſters of the town, headed by their moſt prominent brother, Cotton Mather, led the vaſt crowds in prayer. So impressive was Mather's extemporaneous sermon that he was obliged to attempt to recollect it and commit it to writing that the universal desire for its publication might be satisfied.

A religious revival seems to have occurred, for in the twelve months ending with the month of Mather's death, seventy-one people had become members of his church, among them his dear Nancy. That Nancy could have waited until she was thirty before joining the church speaks well for her father. None of his children was forced in this or any other matter. Katherine, who later died of consumption, joined the church at twenty-four. No child of his was forced into marriage, or an uncongenial occupation, or religion. In a day when parental authority had every sanction of society and church this bespeaks a sweet temper and a wide tolerance. The two of his fifteen children who survived him had memories other than those of their contemporaries; for their father's views of discipline, education, and parenthood were such as to place him among the most enlightened of present-day educators. He was more concerned with awaking a desire to learn, a desire to please, a desire to obey, than to compel compliance to his dictates.

When he felt death approach he wrote to one of his physicians: " My last Enemy is come; I would say, my Best Friend." Death to the Puritan was a dramatic moment. Now all that a godly man had lived for was about to be realized. Now he could hope with supreme emphasis to sum up his life's experience in one effective utterance, and to step into the living presence of God. Cotton Mather stood mentally aloof watching his own death — himself not an unworthy successor to the worthy men he had seen die: Richard Mather bidding his son adieu; that son Increase Mather bidding his son farewell; and now that son himself. His final scene must equal theirs in dignity; he must once more and finally show himself worthy of his ancestry. He had followed his fathers into the ministry; he was following them now into eternity. He saw himself lying on the stately bed; he savored the drama of the scene as he called his son and his nephew. Asked by his son for one final word of inspiration, one by which he could be held in memory, he pronounced firmly " *Fructuosus* " (fruitful).

His congregation, however, did not share his resignation. Desiring to avert this " most awful frown of heaven," they set apart an afternoon for " humble, penitent, and earnest supplications to God our Saviour, that our Pastor may be restored unto usefulness, and continue to be a rich blessing." His death the day after his sixty-fifth birthday they considered " an awful and humbling providence " which not even the assistance of such worthy ministers as Colman, Thatcher, and Sewall in their day of prayer had averted.

The funeral was large, but not without a dash of undignified recrimination, for, recorded his friend Samuel Sewall: " Monday, Febr. 19. Dr. Cotton Mather is intombed; Bearers, The Rev'd Mr. Colman, Mr. Thacher; Mr. Sewall, Prince; Mr. Webb, Cooper. The Church went before the Corps. First the Rev'd Mr. Gee in Mourning alone, then 3 Deacons, then Capt. Hutchinson, Adam Winthrop esqr, Col. Hutchinson — Went up Hull-Street. I went in a Coach. All the Council had Gloves; I had a pair. It seems when the Mourners return'd to the House, Mr. Walter said, My Brother had better Bearers: Mr. Prince answer'd They bore the better part. Mr. Walter pray'd excellently."

Now in the eulogies which flowed from all sides, ministers and journalists vying with each other for first place in praising, all honors were accorded Cotton Mather. His D.D., his F.R.S., his literary skill, his ministerial success, his " universal learning, exalted piety, and extensive charity, his entertaining wit, and singular goodness of temper "; " The capacity of his mind; the readiness of his wit . . .; the strength of his memory; the variety and treasure of his learning . . .; the splendor of virtues . . .; his uncommon activity in the service of Christ "; his affability, his piety, his tolerance — there were not words enough to describe him adequately or to yield him richly deserved honors.

Benjamin Colman, whose friend he had been for years despite Colman's position as pastor of the church of his enemies, was most ready with praises for this man who was, he felt, " The *first minister in the town;* the first in age, in gifts, and in grace," and the most learned in New England from the very time of its foundation.

With all due discount for the general tendency to speak extravagantly of the dead, it must be conceded that Cotton Mather's supposed loss of prestige was but the invention of his enemies and the figment of a tortured mind. He had started his career as a promising young man about whose shoulders clung the mantle of his saintly ancestors; he ended his career with that promise amply fulfilled.

One can but hope that he woke to find himself in that golden heaven the existence of which he doubted least of all as he approached its portals.

CHAPTER EIGHT

"My Life is almost a continual conversation
with Heaven."

— *Diary of Cotton Mather*

IT is one of the paradoxes of Chriſtianity that he who
takes it literally is always looked at askance. At beſt,
if he is willing to retire from the world, he becomes a
saint, a position which, however glorious after canonization, is likely to be diſturbing while the odor of sanctity
is ſtill faint. The man who, despite his religious yearnings,
ſtill aspires to be of the world, usually ends by making
himself somewhat ridiculous. Religion is not unlike literature; the great books of a period are often mere food for
schoolboys within a century; and the religion of the
leaders of one century may in another be the religion of
the inarticulate backwoods. It is therefore useless to say
for Cotton Mather that he honeſtly tried to live a complete and literal Chriſtian life as the Calviniſts defined it;
no one now intereſted in hiſtorical judgment is a Calvin-
iſt. To the Fundamentaliſts Cotton Mather would be a
saint, if Fundamentaliſts had much knowledge of colonial
Massachusetts; to the ordinary man of today he is an incomprehensible figure, one who actually prayed and
faſted in full literal belief that God would hear him.
When Cotton Mather cried to his dying father: " This
Day thou shalt be in Paradise. Do you Believe it, Syr,

and Rejoice in the Views and Hopes of it? " it is foolish
to assume that he did not mean exactly what he said. And
yet for meaning that, he is looked upon by the liberal
Protestants who have made the Mather tradition, as
somewhat soft-brained. By the middle of the eighteenth
century the Massachusetts churches were galloping toward Unitarianism. In 1740 Tutor Flynt of Harvard
wrote of the evangelist Whitefield with the cool con-
descension that even then characterized his Alma Mater:
" He has the old New England and Puritanic way of
thinking and preaching about regeneration and conversion, and justification by faith alone, original sin, etc."
It is clear that Tutor Flynt, but twelve years after Mather's
death, held to a newer and more graceful way of salvation.

Today we have even vaguer definitions of religion than
eighteenth-century Harvard liberals. Our religion tends
to regard society, not the individual. " Doing good "
may be the aim of the modern minister as it was Cotton
Mather's, but it is a doing good in some collective, incorporated way. To Mather doing good was an individual
matter; the social sciences had not yet been discovered.
The most important thing in the world was the soul of
the individual, and the most important thing for that soul
was ultimate union with God. And that ultimate union
could be secured, as far as mere man could hope to secure
it, only through fasting, prayer, a complete faith, and a
moral life. This belief was not confined to the clergy.
Gay men of the world relied implicitly upon its truth.
It was in sober earnest that the merry bookseller Dunton
wrote to his father-in-law: " And to yourself, Sir, I am

bold to say, That I owe all the Blessings of my Life to the many Fasts that you have kept on my Account, and to the many Prayers of my Dearest Wife."

That Cotton Mather fasted some four hundred and fifty times and that he felt at these times in direct communication with God was to him the consequence of a living Christianity; to men of the twentieth century it is an interesting case for abnormal psychology.

The faith which Cotton Mather held so firmly was his by inheritance and by training. He was never under any stress to leave it or to modify it; he felt it his duty to cling to it with a loving intensity because it had belonged to men who had borne witness to its truth with their lives. The evidence in its favor was overwhelming. In his boyhood he had been blessed by men who had crossed the sea for Christ, and as he grew up he felt it an honored burden to leave the religion of his ancestors as pure as he had received it. His task was that of the conservator, an unhonored task in a spendthrift world. The less honor accrues to him for his defense of the old faith because modern men count it a victory to have humbled that faith. There is a good deal of significance in the fact that it was from the pulpit of Cotton Mather's church that Ralph Waldo Emerson stepped down forever from the Congregational ministry.

Cotton Mather could claim none of the glory that comes to the man who fights his way through shadows to the light. From birth he was conditioned to his religion. His zeal, his fastings, his ecstasies can all be paralleled in the diary of his father. Increase Mather wrote: " This morning I experiencd inexpressible meltings of soul, with persuasions that God has work for me to do in England, and that there I shall glorify the dear name of Jesus Chriſt "; and again: " God has vouchsafed to deal familiarly with a poor sinful creature. . . . Marvellous meltings of the soul I did this morning experience with reſpe&ct to tidings from England." This religion Cotton Mather used as his father always used it, to rationalize his desires. There were very few things in Cotton Mather's life for which he could not somehow secure God's warrant that what he wanted badly to do was for God's greater glory. When this warrant had been secured, his enemies, by very simple reasoning, became enemies of God and persecutors of the righteous. This unconscious process of rationalization caused him many an aching hour. God had manifeſtly commanded so many plantings which never bore fruit that at times all Mather's attempts to do good seemed to come to nothing.

As a result there grew up in him a firſt-rate persecution complex. Never was a man so pursued by the devil as he. The malignity which surrounded him was inexplicable. The death of his wives and children were, of course, due to God's inscrutable dispensations. Of such chaſtenings he could say: " Tis a Thought full of Consolation to me, and that carries an Animation of Piety with it; that the sad Things which appear to me, as Punishments of my Offences, and I accordingly Accept them, and I don't complain, but say, I will bear the Indignation of the Lord, because I have sinned againſt him; they really prove Benefits unto me, and I find them intended for such; and they have those precious Effects upon me, which proclame the everlasting Love of God unto me." But for the malevolence of men there was no such cheerful explanation. A few years before his death he felt that he had reached the end of a passage; at a meeting of ministers he declared that his efforts to do good had made the world " really too hott a Place for me to continue in." He went on: " The most false Representations imaginable have been made of me; and of my Conduct. . . . *I have done! I have done! I have done* treating you with any more of my Proposals. If they should be never so good, yett if they be known to be mine, that is enough to bespeak a Blast upon them. Do *you* propose as many good Things as you please, and I will second them, and assist them and fall in with them, to the best of my Capacity."

In a man of fifty-nine this was not petulance. It was a settled conviction that " cruel Hatred," " personal Revenges," and " villainous Abuses " were his lot in life, the natural interpretation of one who suffered from an ambition to do greater things than life permitted him to accomplish. This sense of frustration was always with him. It is not fanciful to connect it with his lifelong devotion to his father. Increase Mather absorbed his son none the less because unconsciously. Cotton Mather never really had a chance to strike out for himself; little that really mattered in his life was of his own making: his political activity, his quarrels, his religion, his church, his literary activity, — everything followed his father's fashioning. His independent fight for smallpox inoculation, which should have brought him glory, brought merely

[260]

abuse and bitterness. One need not pursue modern analysis to the limit and suggest that his constant anxiety that his father be prepared for death — years before Increase's eighty-four years were done he seemed to his son to have his wings spread for a flight to heaven — was due to an unthought and unrecognized wish to escape from his father's shadow; it is kinder to look at the words of Increase in his will: " Concerning my Son Cotton Mather He has bin a great Comfort to me from his Childhood, having bin a very dutiful Son, and a singular Blessing to his Father's Family and Flock." And the son no less than the father knew fully that it was Increase's flock.

With Cotton Mather's sense of frustration were mingled, perhaps necessarily, a passion for service to men and for abasement before God, a craving for honors mingled with the overwhelming desire to do something to deserve them. Life seemed to him worth living only as it brought recognition of his efforts to live gloriously; he valued the opinion of the world enough to believe that if recognition were not forthcoming it was a sure sign that he had failed.

The astonishing thing is that instead of vanity and overwhelming conceit, this attitude produced an extraordinary ingenuity in self-depreciation. Surely no man in 1724 who knew Cotton Mather as the most famous preacher in Massachusetts, who knew his honors from abroad, his scores of distinguished correspondents, his social influence, his fame as the author of hundreds of publications, who knew him as the foremost among New England intellectuals, constantly quoted, always in demand as a preacher whether at the ordination of blessed ministers or the execution of blasphemous pirates, no contemporary would have assumed that at this very time he was brooding over " some very *dark Dispensations.*" After all he had done for sailors, he reflected, " In *Prayers* for them; in *Sermons* to them; in *Books* bestow'd on them," yet " there is not a Man in the world, so Reviled, so slandered, so cursed, among the Sailors." He had helped negroes, and yet negroes were named Cotton-Mather so that their masters might " with some Shadow of Truth, assert Crimes as committed by one of that Name, which the Hearers take to be *me.*" He had not enough psychology to realize that even slander is a form of flattery; stories do not grow about unimportant men. He had done much for " the Profit and Honour of the *female Sex,* yet there are not twenty women in the town " but have at some time or other spoken basely of him. And so with his relatives, his children, Scotchmen, the government, Harvard College, which " could not easily show [him] more Contempt " if he were " the greatest Blockhead that ever came from it," his friends, his books, his charity — all the good that he had done ended in his being " by far the most afflicted minister in all *New-England.*" Such a recital is the outlet used by all sufferers from an inferiority complex, complete wallowing in grief.

The modern reader would be more sympathetic if he felt that Cotton Mather had really any power of critical analysis. His world regarded him as an immensely learned man; and that part of his reputation is still more solidly based than any other. His ſtaggering bibliography of four hundred and thirty-seven items, the huge variety of his information, the mere quantity of matter in his *Magnalia* — all this weight makes of him with Benjamin Franklin and Jonathan Edwards one of the three indispensable figures in even a cursory sketch of American literature. But his learning was like his enormously busy life, like the hundreds of pages of notes of benevolent intentions that gush out over his diary. What is lacking is the power to see into the heart of things. Cotton Mather's learning, like his " good devices," is purely superficial. It shows no power of analysis, no sense for the interrelation of cause and effeét, no critical judgment, none of the simple discrimination of common sense. His curiosity was immense, but it was not scientific. The mind that swallows all physical phenomena without syſtem, without scepticism, which believes that all manifeſtations of the invisible world are visible, which cannot separate the credible from the incredible, which has no feeling for evidence or authorities, such a mind — and it was the common mind of Cotton Mather's time — may be encyclopedic, or quaint, or ſtaggering, but it is not scientific. Science depends upon a recognition of law and method, of adequate causes and inevitable results; it is searching, critical, sceptical, methodical. Aside from a body of faéts which are indispensable to the ſtudent of colonial hiſtory, there is nothing in the enormous work of Cotton Mather that the world really treasures. There is nothing like Franklin's autobiography or Jonathan Edwards' relentless sermons. What is reprinted is intereſting because it

[263]

throws light upon Cotton Mather's personality, because it illustrates a reputation which has been only dimly traditional, not because it is intrinsically valuable. One can make out a case for some of the lives in the *Magnalia* and for some of the passages in the sermons, but the case is hardly for these passages as literary art. The fact is that Cotton Mather is a man of letters only in the text-books of literature. What he published he published for a purpose, to bolster up a waning tradition, to glorify God, to be useful, to do good. The writers of utilitarian prose are sometimes artists by accident, but seldom by intention. There are certainly passages in Cotton Mather which are clear, forceful, rhythmical, and effective, but there is certainly no evidence that he valued these purely artistic qualities, and they bulk large in the immense body of his work only in the minds of his apologists. In the history of American thought he is a towering figure, though as an illustration, not as an influence; in the history of American literature one will find him, in general, merely quaint and curious.

When one examines Cotton Mather in the light of contemporary criticism, one finds him curiously lacking in historical charm. In all the hosts of references in diaries, letters, and records, even in his own voluminous diary, one rarely sees him as a dramatic figure. He is never in an attitude like the immortal Pemberton, passionately " capering with his feet," as he bitterly upbraids Samuel Sewall for subserviency to the Mathers; he is never a dramatic figure like Dudley, lashing the impudent farmer and roaring, " You lie, you dog, you lie, you divell."

Once he almoſt achieves drama as he rides his white horse among the crowd at Burroughs's execution; but the ſtory reſts upon Calef's slender authority. Once there is a scrap of holy conversation, but only once; otherwise one muſt use one's imagination. The flicker of daily life on the screen, the nameless unremembered aĉts, the passing of seasons, the recreations of his family, food, pleasure, the thousand incidents which give a sense of a peopled world — all these are lacking. Only once or twice in his lengthy diary does he pause to comment on the beauty of spring. Only twice does he phrase or indicate any philosophical reflĉection — and then it is only the uses of adversity and the vanity of labor, the former being a passionate part of his creed, the latter merely a passing petulance. Only his spiritual life remains, and with the passing of two centuries that has loſt much of its passionate reality.

In considering Cotton Mather's relations with his contemporaries, therefore, one muſt analyze rather than dramatize. Was he right? Was he fair? Was he unselfish? Some things are certain: he was impulsive and reckless; he was entirely naïve in his assumption that the purity of his motives would always be recognized; he judged before he inveſtigated; and where his father was attacked, or what he conceived to be religious truth was assailed, he loſt all power of reflĉection. Certainly he was seldom taĉtful, and he possessed to a remarkable degree the power of putting himself in the wrong. And yet one muſt acquit him of all meanness, chicanery, trickery, and falsehood. He was thoroughly honeſt and thoroughly faithful to his

[265]

ſtandards. The greateſt bar to hiſtorical sympathy is the proud isolation in which both he and his father lived, without intimates, though with scores of friends, secure in brahminical remoteness.

His inner private life, the life of his dreams, ambitions, and emotions, he has revealed more completely than any other American. His diary is not, like Samuel Sewall's, a record of what happened; it is a record of what he felt.

Perhaps the moſt ſtriking thing to a modern reader is the renewed confirmation which it gives to the intimate conneĉtion between religious fervor and sexual hyperæſthesia. It is clear that Mather lived in a ſtate of tremulous sensitiveness to the brushing of angels' wings. Conſtant residence in one place, conſtant reading, ſtudy, and writing, conſtant preaching in a ſtate of exalted excitement, conſtant brooding over the sins of his parishioners, sins which it was his duty to examine and censure — all this, years on end with comparatively slight relief, kept him in a condition of excited tension. In marriage he found some relief. Yet after his fiftieth year marriage aggravated rather than palliated his troubles, and toward the end of his life he approached pretty close to morbidity. Certainly he was acutely nervous, high-ſtrung, and "jumpy." As he saw an enemy in every man, so he saw himself in every sinner. What he needed was relief, but he could never "cleanse his bosom of . . . perilous stuff." A single inſtance will show how his mind seethed with the burden of his parishioners' sins:

On May 3, 1718, " A very wicked Woman is found in the Church whereof I am the Servant. She not only had an unlawful Offspring a few Years ago, which is now discovered, but her Impenitence has provoked her Neighbours to come in with Testimonies of a very lewd Conversation, that she has carried on." This is bad enough, but it brings with it the inevitable persecution. " But her Father, who is an old and great Professor of Religion, does most grievously misbehave himself on this Occasion. He, and his foolish Family do not only treat me very ill . . . but also, they use violent Wayes to sow Discord among the Neighbours, and the Peace of the Church is threatened." Whereupon comes the inevitable self-abasement: " I would bewayl the Sins of my People, as being on some Accounts my own. . . . At the same Time, I am attended with various Difficulties, and marvellous Temptations, (whereof one is, I hope, this day happily conquered,) that call me to ly in the dust before the Lord." It is impossible to doubt that he dramatized himself in the sins of his flock and that his vicarious sinning brought him variety, at least, from the regularity of life.

A week later he still broods upon the affair and sets apart the day " on the same Ocasions and with the same Exercises, that I was this Day se'ennight before the Lord." Here is the very depth of religious abasement, a tangled complex of emotion: " I meet with very breaking and killing Things," he writes, " which are the Chastisements of the holy God upon me, for my manifold Miscarriages. . . . Now such is my Love unto my God; and so united is my Soul unto Him, that I have a secret Pleasure in my Thoughts of the Gratification which is done unto Him, in the sad Things which tear me to Pieces before Him."

The next week he is before the Lord on the " same Occasions." Now he foresees God's " terrible Vengeance "; he is filled with " inexpressible Agony." On June 4th the case comes before the church. In the church records it appears: " Her Confession was this Day read unto the Brethren of the Church, which foolishly insisted on her total Ignorance of any thing done to give her any Impregnation, the Church unanimously voted, that they could not accept of her Confession." So she was sentenced to admonition and exclusion from Communion. And on June 9th, after more than a month of agony, Cotton Mather writes: " A Discipline to be this day managed in the Church — which I have made many Prayers about. May the glorious Lord help me on this Occasion, to speak such Things as the Flock may fare the better for. The Church proves unanimous." And thus passed another crisis, and for a while there was peace in a troubled soul.

Were his cyclonic emotional outbursts not preserved in his diary the world would know nothing of them. To the world Cotton Mather seemed a happy man who inspired great personal affection. Three women married him and more than one courted him before each of his marriages; two of his wives were women of experience, and one, at least, was a fashionable woman of the world. One gay woman, perhaps the only woman he ever deeply loved, would have married him if she could. It is noteworthy that of his children the one of whom he was passionately fond reveled in all the vices from which a man of God was rigorously excluded. Of his other children he was properly fond. It seems hardly fair, therefore, to hold against him the frank revelation of an emotional life which most of us never fish up from the unconscious. Plenty of other men would show the same record if their powers of introspection were developed as was his.

Even in his diary, however, he was not spontaneous. Except for his later years the entries are none of them first draft. Even in the piteous exclamations over his "wicked son Increase," those recurrent ejaculations "My God! My God!" one is not quite sure that he did not glance over his shoulder to be sure that God was hearing his grief. Mingled with an undoubted naïveté is a certain dramatic quality, an unmistakable desire to interpret himself suitably to the public. He expected his diary to be read. His wives frequently dipped into it — so that he occasionally had to lapse into Latin to prevent their reading certain entries; even into using Greek characters, especially with the word *coniunx,* presumably because the third wife could recognize a little Latin. His son Samuel drank deep draughts from this diary, and with the mere change of "I" to "he" wrote much of his pious life of his father. Had the original entries remained, for all their self-conscious polishing, we should know more than it is now possible to surmise of Mather's feelings during the witchcraft trials. He wrote even in this intimate record for an ultimate reader whose good opinion he desired. He tried always to be correct in his thoughts, his deeds, his emotions. Religious ecstasy, self-abasement, were proper; and so was grief properly restrained. The passionate anger which was spontaneous with him was not proper, and was rarely recorded.

Self-analysis does not make for happiness. It leads into dark and tortured by-paths where every shadow is ill-omened. Objective activity gives a happier life even when most empty. To look ever within, to make important the most trivial acts and thoughts, is to court madness. Cotton Mather, unwilling to lose even a minute of his days, would, while he dressed, consider the various parts of his body and meditate upon the holy uses to which he could put each and every one, upon the ways in which he could glorify God with each. Similarly, he clothed his soul with irradiating thoughts searching each part of that soul with painful scrutiny. It is slight wonder that he constantly found flaws in his thoughts and in his conduct. He was forever berating himself as the most filthy of sinners, the most slothful of worshipers, at the same time that he recorded innumerable fastings, prayers, sermons, and charities. His life, as he wrote, was in the last decade almost " a continual conversation with Heaven "; he strove with a persistence probably never surpassed to make his life conform with that of Jesus Christ. But all his strivings, all his pious thoughts, all his good deeds, remained individual; they were never lifted into the realm of the universal.

Such a man, such a thinker, however great his influence during his lifetime, could never leave a mark on succeeding generations. He did not transmute his experiences into a philosophy of life; he did not translate his emotions into phrases of universal truth.

[270]

He was one who dwelt apart; though he walked with his head in the clouds of pious revery, he yet saw all the mud spots in his path. He looked up and saw spiritual light; he looked down and saw the murkieſt evil. The only relationship he could deduce, the only reason for anything good or bad, was the inscrutable plan of God. One thing only he underſtood: that in eternal life all was light. And he could close his eyes upon life here below with the sure feeling that God was good.

THE END